Best wishes to
    Della + John
  from Kath. Crozier.

# It Was Like This

It Was Like This © Kathleen Crozier July 2004
Front cover picture 'Yo-Yos' by Kathleen Crozier © July 2004
Back cover photograph by Sue Watts © July 2004
For copyright of all other illustrations see page xi

First Published by UPSO August 2004

The author has asserted her right under the Copyright Designs and Patents Act 1988 to be identified as the author of this work.

All rights reserved. No part of this work may be reproduced or stored in an information system, other than for purposes of review, without prior written permission by the copyright holder.

A catalogue record of this book is available from the British Library.

ISBN: 1-84375-108-9

To order additional copies of this book please visit:
http://www.upso.co.uk/kathleencrozier

Published by: UPSO Ltd
5 Stirling Road, Castleham Business Park,
St Leonards-on-Sea, East Sussex TN38 9NW United Kingdom
Tel: 01424 853349 Fax: 0870 1913991
Email: info@upso.co.uk Web: http://www.upso.co.uk

# It Was Like This

by

Kathleen Crozier

UPSO

For my Grandchildren
Rebecca, Emily, Jesse and Isabel

# Acknowledgements

Many thanks for the valuable editorial assistance of: Michael Smith, Sue Watts and Gwenda Lee of the Hastings Writers' Group.

# List of Illustrations

# Acknowledgements

Note: We would like to thank the persons or companies named below who gave permission to reproduce their pictures. Owing to the age of these pictures, it was not always possible to find or contact the original source to obtain such permission. We would like to apologise to any person or company if we have infringed their rights and the author and editors undertake to negotiate any compensation that may be required.

We would also like to make it clear that any such infringement is entirely our responsibility and that the publisher, UPSO, is not liable in any way.

1. Kit Knights aged 2 with brother Lionel
   *Picture by H R Marchant, 52 Bohemia Road, St Leonards-on-Sea.*

2. Middle Street
   *Unknown source.*

3. Five Boys Chocolate Advertisement
   *Reproduced with kind permission of Cadbury Ltd., Copyright holders.*

4. The Fire Station
   *Unknown source.*

5. Perce Knights in his front workshop
   *Copyright Kathleen Crozier.*

6  Fag cards
   *Reproduced with kind permission of Imperial Tobacco Co., Copyright holders.*

7  Kit Knights and family
   *Picture by H R Marchant, 52 Bohemia Road, St Leonards-on-Sea.*

8  Sister Muriel
   *Copyright Kathleen Crozier.*

9  Grandad Bastien
   *Copyright Kathleen Crozier.*

10 Grandma Bastien
   *Copyright Kathleen Crozier.*

11 Uncle Harry and family
   *Picture by Mc Lennan, Freshwater, Isle of Wight.*

12 Aunt Jessie Bastien
   *Picture by A R Perry, 13 Wellington Place, Hastings.*

13 Mum, Carrie Bastien
   *Picture by A R Perry, 13 Wellington Place, Hastings.*

14 On The Good Ship 'Yacki Hicki Doo La'
   *Words and music by Billy Merson © 1917 Francis, Day & Hunter Ltd., London WC2H 0QY*
   *Reproduced by permission of International Music Publications Ltd. All rights reserved.*

15 Map of Middle Street and Cricket Ground
   *Reproduced from O.S. map of 1897.*

16 The Cricket Ground
   *Reproduced with kind permission of the Hastings Museum.*

17 Muriel with cousin Molly
   *Copyright Kathleen Crozier.*

18 The Net Shops
*Copyright Kathleen Crozier.*

19 The Boating Lake, Alexandra Park
*Postcard (sent 4/7/1908) printed by Davidson Bros., London and New York.*

20 Lake with Black Swans, Alexandra Park
*Postcard (sent 28/8/1905) printed by Empire Series, London.*

# FOREWORD

Kathleen Crozier was a teacher until her retirement in 1973.

She then concentrated on her lifelong interests in art and printmaking. A founder member of the Greenwich printmakers, her work is held in collections in the UK, Europe and America. Her paintings have also been exhibited in The Royal Academy and The Royal Society of Painters and Etchers. The front cover of this book and illustration 17 on page 96 are examples of her early work.

On the death of her husband, Kathleen moved back to Hastings and continued with her numerous local activities. Apart from holding frequent exhibitions of her artwork, and ceramics, she also joined the Anglo-French Club and the Hastings Writers' Group. Examples of her early writing are in the addendum of this book.

We first met Kathleen when she joined the Writers' Group some ten years ago. Her creative writing ability and outspoken views rapidly earned the respect, admiration and friendship of the members.

Three years ago, Kathleen moved into Old Hastings House. However, she was determined to continue with her artistic and literary interests. Last year she decided to write her childhood memoirs for the benefit of her grandchildren and asked us to help with the typing and preparation of a booklet.

After the first few instalments it became apparent that these lively and entertaining memoirs deserved a wider audience. Hence the idea of a published book was born.

During the production of this book we constantly bore in mind that it was *Kathleen's* memoirs and that we would make as few editorial changes as possible. Moreover, any change would only be made with Kathleen's approval. Therefore, the text is almost exactly as her original manuscript and any editorial corrections are with her approval.

The final result is, we hope, not only of value to her family, but also of interest to anyone concerned with the history of Hastings, or the social history of working class life at the beginning of the twentieth century. Indeed, we believe the book is a very good read in its own right.

We hope you as the reader agree with us.

# CONTENTS

**Our Street** . . . . . . . . . . . . . . . . . . . . . . . . . . . . . . . . 1
   Middle Street, Hastings . . . . . . . . . . . . . . . . . . . 2

**Street Activities** . . . . . . . . . . . . . . . . . . . . . . . . . . . 21
   Street Games . . . . . . . . . . . . . . . . . . . . . . . . . . . . 21
   Fag Cards . . . . . . . . . . . . . . . . . . . . . . . . . . . . . . 26
   Marbles . . . . . . . . . . . . . . . . . . . . . . . . . . . . . . . 28
   More about Horses . . . . . . . . . . . . . . . . . . . . . . . 29
   Visitors to the Street . . . . . . . . . . . . . . . . . . . . . . 30

**Home and Family** . . . . . . . . . . . . . . . . . . . . . . . . . 33
   My Home . . . . . . . . . . . . . . . . . . . . . . . . . . . . . . 33
   Indoor Occupations . . . . . . . . . . . . . . . . . . . . . . . 38
   Books and Reading . . . . . . . . . . . . . . . . . . . . . . . 44
   The Knights . . . . . . . . . . . . . . . . . . . . . . . . . . . . 44
   The Bastiens . . . . . . . . . . . . . . . . . . . . . . . . . . . . 48
   Clothes . . . . . . . . . . . . . . . . . . . . . . . . . . . . . . . . 57
   Food . . . . . . . . . . . . . . . . . . . . . . . . . . . . . . . . . . 60
   Early Christmases . . . . . . . . . . . . . . . . . . . . . . . . 61
   Neighbours . . . . . . . . . . . . . . . . . . . . . . . . . . . . 66

**Outside Activities** . . . . . . . . . . . . . . . . . . . . . . . . . 69
   Organisations . . . . . . . . . . . . . . . . . . . . . . . . . . . 69
   School - St Mary in the Castle . . . . . . . . . . . . . . . 72
   Sundays, Religion and Church . . . . . . . . . . . . . . . 77
   Entertainments . . . . . . . . . . . . . . . . . . . . . . . . . . 79
   Shops and Shopping . . . . . . . . . . . . . . . . . . . . . . 86

**Surrounding Areas** . . . . . . . . . . . . . . . . . . . . . . . . . . . . . 89
    The Cricket Ground. . . . . . . . . . . . . . . . . . . . . . . . . . 89
    The West Hill . . . . . . . . . . . . . . . . . . . . . . . . . . . . . . 90
    East Hill . . . . . . . . . . . . . . . . . . . . . . . . . . . . . . . . . 91
    Ecclesbourne and Fairlight Glens . . . . . . . . . . . . . . . . 92
    The Sea . . . . . . . . . . . . . . . . . . . . . . . . . . . . . . . . . . 94
    The Catholic Grounds . . . . . . . . . . . . . . . . . . . . . . . 98
    Alexandra Park to Old Roar . . . . . . . . . . . . . . . . . . 99
    The Brassey Institute . . . . . . . . . . . . . . . . . . . . . . . 103

**The War 1914-1918** . . . . . . . . . . . . . . . . . . . . . . . . . . 107
    Finale. . . . . . . . . . . . . . . . . . . . . . . . . . . . . . . . . . 110

**To My Family** . . . . . . . . . . . . . . . . . . . . . . . . . . . . . . 113

**Addendum** . . . . . . . . . . . . . . . . . . . . . . . . . . . . . . . . 115
    Lament for a Space. . . . . . . . . . . . . . . . . . . . . . . . 115
    Under the Pier . . . . . . . . . . . . . . . . . . . . . . . . . . . 117
    Down in the Govers . . . . . . . . . . . . . . . . . . . . . . . 118
    A M Stonham . . . . . . . . . . . . . . . . . . . . . . . . . . . 120
    The P & P Boards . . . . . . . . . . . . . . . . . . . . . . . . 122
    In the Hop Gardens . . . . . . . . . . . . . . . . . . . . . . . 124

# Our Street

This is the story of a place, a period, and an unattractive small girl. The place is a South Coast town, the time 1908 onwards, and the child, myself – Kit Knights in those days.

*Illustration 1 - Kit Knights aged two with brother Lionel*

## Middle Street, Hastings

My earliest strong memories are of our street rather than the home. And what a street – a mini-metropolis. It was narrow, busy and fairly dirty because of the horse traffic. It was not very long but contained enough goings on and play places to make it not urgent to go further afield to the beaches or the hills. Though when you were a little older, there they were, waiting for you.

The horse droppings didn't stay long because there was always some kid quick enough to dash in with a bucket and shovel to gather it up while still steaming, for a grateful parent or neighbour. "Do you want some dung, Mum? Give us the shovel." The word manure was not in anyone's vocabulary in those days.

At the very bottom, facing the end of the street, was the Police Station, a solid Victorian stone building which appeared to strike no terror in our hearts as we often poked our noses inside the outer door to see what was going on. Beyond it was the Town Hall, which we didn't count as ours because there was no access from our side, only from the main road.

Next to the Police Station was a quickie, in and out men's lavatory, which was no concern of mine, but useful for the boys to hide in when a girl was 'he' in interminable games of Tegger. As a matter of fact there was a slightly more commodious lavatory next door to the Town Hall, which I explored one day because I didn't see why I should be kept out if I chose to go in, and I was curious to see what they looked like inside. I had no form of comparison because, in those days, there were no such things as public ladies' lavatories. I was surprised to find no seats and a constant trickle of water down the green walls into a gutter – and they stank! I must have been about seven by then as I was able to read. I could not understand my mother's anger when I asked her at dinner-time the meaning of 'Adjust your dress before leaving'. It seemed silly because people with dresses didn't go in there.

Coming back to the street, it started with a pub, not frequented by my father and therefore despised – so we ran in and out of the front passage and shouted with a clear conscience. I think it was called The Clarence. (It is still there.) Next to it came the large building, almost a courtyard in fact, which was a great amenity. This was Payne Rogers – a kind of wholesale fruit and veg market for the whole town. In front of this, large carts with metal-rimmed wheels, the forerunners of today's juggernauts, were always standing or going or coming, from early morning till midday, pulled by large horses with big feet which you early learned to dodge. Men stood on the carts (looking gigantic) and threw down boxes and bags of produce brought in from the surrounding countryside. The horses and the men were friendly as long as you didn't get in their way. The noise of hoofs and wheels and raucous male voices was amazing. The smell of rotten apples, outside leaves of cabbages and soggy onions lingered on till after the gutter was swept out and the smaller carts and handcarts of the retailers had left. It was no Covent Garden, but it seemed immense to us.

One delightful day my mother allowed me to go with another girl in the street (whose Grandad Downe was a driver) out on a job. We drove as far as Appledore right out into Kent, mounted high, and quietly delirious with joy, fresh air and self-importance. Mum was a bit dubious; she thought Alice Picknell and her mother, common, or 'no cop', but she liked old man Downe – 'he was a gentleman'. More of them as we get further up the street.

Opposite the market was a boring blank wall – the side of a dreary but important grey building facing the police station road. It had a shiny brass plate at the front with 'Commissioner for Oaths' written on it, another puzzler for me, and for Mum when I asked her what an oath was. She said it was a swear word and where did I get that from? I wondered why there should be a special shop or office where you could go to buy or learn swear words! A puzzling world for little girls who could read. I didn't ask about the word 'Commissioner' because I wasn't absolutely sure how to say it – and I could not bear to be laughed at. Had I asked, no doubt Mum would have realised what I was on about.

I think the Drill Hall must have come next to the market; at any rate I can remember a brick wall with no windows on the ground floor, which eventually declared its identity by a wide white Gothic arch filled with wood which could be opened down the middle as two great curved gates on suitable occasions, but usually gave access by a normal-sized door cut out of them. You had to lift your feet when you went in because the opening did not quite reach to the ground. First timers often caught their toe on this bottom four inches of wood and entered head first, to our joy, and those who only staggered and clutched the side tended to lose their temper. Much happened in the Drill Hall, war-like celebrations, children's parties and so on.

The red brick continued equally far beyond the central door until it reached a small pub, The Volunteer, the smallest but most important because it was the local for the street. The Volunteer was a little ale-house across the street and slightly below us, next to the 'banana factory' and my grandma's cottage. It was tiny, with one small and dusty bar into which most of the men of the street crowded in the evening, but in the daytime it was empty. Beside it was a narrow corridor with a small hatch into the bar, and here the women of the neighbourhood could pop in discreetly carrying a jug, often covered by a cloth. Even my lady-like little grandma in her lavender coloured blouse, lace-collared and with black sateen apron carefully covering her jug, could be seen at times going into the 'Jug and Bottle' department, hoping that no-one would notice such a short public sally.

'Chucking out time' came when I was in bed, still awake but dozing. I would often hear the murmuration of voices and the opening and closing of doors. As they were turned out of the pub, mellow and merry, but sober, a knot of men always gathered on the pavement and rhubarbed away for about half an hour. Loud guffaws and exclamations of "Good ol' Perce" and similar appreciative remarks punctuated the sound of a quieter voice, which was obviously telling a good story. Old Perce was a great storyteller. He was also my dad.

So with only a few buildings we are a third of the way up the street and rapidly approaching my grandma's. Between The Volunteer and her house was only one small dwelling, then another wide wooden gate which shut off a small yard leading to a large shed. I can't remember what this hid when I was tiny, but quite early Payne Rogers took this over and made it their 'banana factory'.

As for the 'banana factory', as a small child I never saw a banana at all; I don't think they were eaten in this country, or if they were they must have been rare and probably expensive. The first ones I ever saw were small and deeper yellow and were known as Canaries because that was where they came from. They were certainly of superior flavour, but as the years went by and the big ones gained a hold, they seemed to fade out. We knew of course that Payne Rogers did not actually make bananas in their factory. We watched the men with sacks over their heads carrying great hands of green fruit in, but curiously I never saw them brought out again. Perhaps they were cut up into smaller bunches when ripe and the retailers backed small carts right into the yard. We were never able to get beyond the gates, which were always locked when the men weren't carrying – so what form of warmth, if any, was used to ripen the fruit, I can't say. It must have been pretty primitive.

Even from my gran's back bedroom window you could see nothing, yet she lived next door. It was not a big affair, but it brought its own excitement. Often strange creatures emerged from the great clusters of fruit, and these

*Illustration 2 - Middle Street. Early morning milk delivery.
Within a few hours this almost deserted scene would be a hive of activity*

the men usually took home to annoy their families and girl friends. Dad several times brought in enormous black spiders with thick hairy legs, about six inches across. Both delight and terror were felt, and squeals and yells were uttered in our little kitchen, especially by Mum, and we all firmly believed they were tarantulas and that, if bitten, we would go mad and never be able to stop dancing. What happened to these exotic unfortunates when they had finished showing their paces, being diverted away from ourselves with a gentle push of a stick or toe, I don't know, but I imagine they went down the lavatory. The rumours of snakes, scorpions and other monsters were rife, and I suppose this explains why Payne Rogers was probably the only building in the street that hadn't been explored by the children.

So let's go back where we started, to the bottom of the street but on the other side, by the grim featureless cement building of the Commissioner for Oaths. Alongside was a house door which opened direct on to a flight of stairs. This seemed most odd – where were the downstairs rooms? Fancy having to go upstairs to the kitchen! Flats were not much in evidence in those days and then only in circumstances similar to this. I suppose these rooms went over the premises next door. This flat was occupied by one of my mother's 'perfect gentlemen'. She was a great connoisseur of gentlemen and I always, without understanding the qualifications necessary, took her word for it. He was a nice quiet man called Mr Pound, with pure white hair and moustache and a broad-brimmed trilby hat. He could have been in his fifties, and was only to be seen going to and from work at Draycon's.

He had a daughter Grace who was still at school and presumably looked after her dad. I thought her grown up, dignified and fascinating. An arrangement had been made that when I was five Grace should take me to school. No-one else in the street appealed so to my mum. She wore a blouse, a long skirt and a straw hat, and had her hair tied back with a big black bow. I was so proud of being entrusted to Grace, though I cannot ever remember so much as speaking to her. I did get taken up those stairs once, probably on the occasion when Mum and Mr Pound came to their arrangement on my behalf. Alas, I never got the thrill of walking hand in hand with Grace up Queens Road, because I didn't actually get to school till I was six and what happened to Grace I don't know. She must have arrived at the great age of twelve or thirteen and gone out into the big world as a shop assistant or skivvy.

The Pound's rooms must have been over the lock-up premises of Mitchel and Thunder, the newspaper wholesaler for the town. The rolling gates were pushed up very early by a long pole with a metal hook on the end and finished up at the top with a clang. Some of the earliest little motor-vans tore down from the station, their back doors were flung open, great bales of newspapers were slung out roughly, counted, broken up, flung from one corner of the premises to the other and repacked on to handcarts and bicycles or into newsboys' bags, to be disseminated all over the town. A small pile of each was taken to the shop two doors further up and that's where we were sent to buy them.

What a generous array of choices: Daily Express, News Chronicle, Daily News, Times, Telegraph, Mirror, Sketch, Daily Herald, Daily Mail, and a racing paper, Lloyd's News. And the Sundays: Times, Mirror, Sketch, Sunday Express, the Reynolds News, and the News of the World. Then there were the weeklies: Chips, John o' London, John Bull, Answers, Titbits, Magnet, Gem (fourpence), The Union Jack (featuring Sexton Blake and Tinker his boy assistant, later to become a monthly magazine called The Sexton Blake Library), The Boys' Own Paper and the Scout.

Again, as long as we didn't get that much in the way of the workmen, get hit by bales, or get in the path of their short sharp knives, which inscribed a swift and dangerous arc when cutting the ropes, nobody seemed to mind us. And there was the added attraction that you might well get away with some useful pieces of hemp or single sheets of last week's comics used to wrap the bales. That wholesaler moved fairly soon, but only up to the top of the street which was that much nearer the station. It was also adjoining the house of the Sellens family, from which Siddie will appear later as my only sweetheart.

Now we go back down to the bottom and there between Thunder's wholesale premises and the retail paper shop was the more refined of the two sweet shops in the street. It was three steps up, very clean, and the street children hardly ever used it. When my 'rich' auntie and uncle came down from London and wished to buy us some sweets, that's where we went. A bell over the doorway pinged, and we never ever spoke a word. It seemed such a superior place. I imagine that our normal currency of halfpennies and farthings did not attract the affection of the proprietors, so that in some way they must have succeeded in keeping us out. The best things in this shop were whipped cream walnuts (twopence for one sweet!) and bars of Fry's chocolate cream, marked off into six divisions and filled with insidiously sweet squashy cream. They were in fact not quite so thrilling as the enamel plaque screwed to the front door. This showed the five somewhat revolting little boys in sailor suits; their faces contorted with feelings ranging through anger and greed to self-satisfaction.

I loved that advertisement and if ever some adult treated me, an unusual proceeding in those days, it was their bar of chocolate that I chose – at twopence. Unfortunately, because of its soft centre it disappeared very quickly and left behind sticky face and fingers.

Then there was an alley with a locked rusty iron gate, leading I suppose to the back way of the sweet shop. After that came Thunder's retail shop which was incredibly dim and dusty, but friendly. I can remember another moment of embarrassment connected with that. After I was compulsorily joined to the Brownies by my brother and his cohorts, I was greatly excited

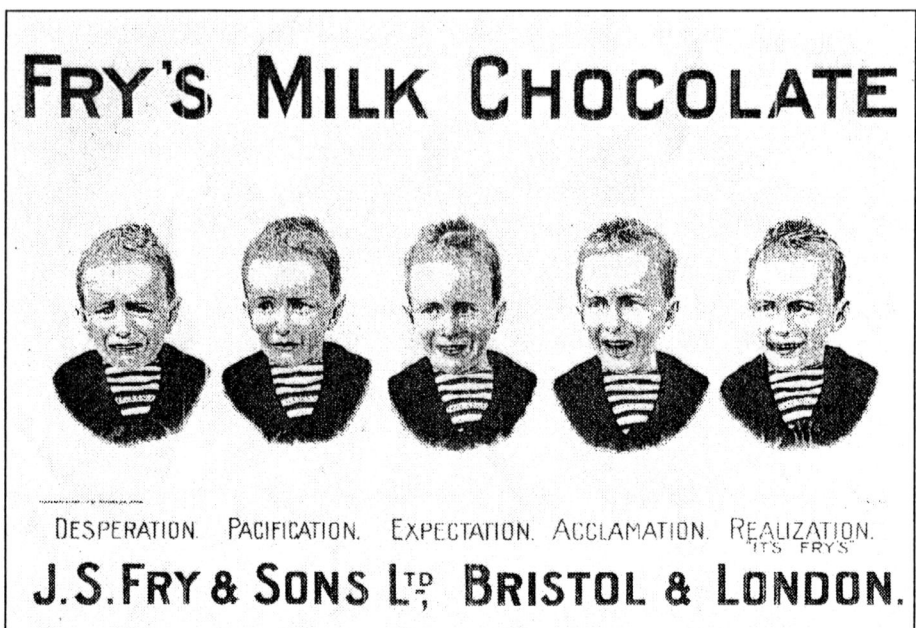

*Illustration 3 - Reproduced by kind permission of Cadbury Ltd*

by the announcement that a weekly called The Guide was to be launched. For once I must have made my yearnings clear to my family, instead of smothering them. I was a child who never asked for any money to be expended on her, vaguely realising that we hadn't any for superfluities. Dad agreed that I could have at least the first number and see how we got on. Down I went to Thunder's and put in my order for about a fortnight ahead when the new magazine was billed to appear. Every day seemed an aeon, but at last a strange pink paper appeared on the doorstep, tucked into the Daily Express. Where was my copy of The Guide; what was this paper? The biggest word on the title banner was definitely Guide but the thing was full of columns of numbers, times and mysterious names. I took it in and my parents were at first very annoyed – what would the neighbours think? Thunder would soon blow it about that Perce Knights had suddenly taken to buying the Racing Guide. Meanwhile I wept with chagrin, both on account of the waste and my parents' crossness, followed by Dad's guffaws. I was convinced I had made a dreadful blunder and no-one had the sense to point out that I hadn't. It was simply that the wholesaler had been dealing with Racing Guide for years, and didn't all that much cater for little girls.

Anyway when I did eventually get hold of my anticipated Guide I found it so feeble and girly and full of washing up and helping old ladies across roads, that I never wanted to see it again. All my young life I was chagrined by the sheer awfulness and boredom of any toys or books turned out for girls. So I stuck to The Boys' Own Paper and Scouting for Boys, and became a kind of miniature surrogate male, encouraged by the closeness of my brother and the chivalrous way in which his friends always accepted my presence in the gang.

I contented myself with the odd copies of the Gem and the Magnet (both forbidden by my parents as dross) and of Comic Cuts, Chips, Mutt & Geoff and the occasional Sexton Blake and Tinker story. Not once did we ever buy one or have one bought for us, but somehow we acquired them.

Next up the street was a most important business, the fish and chip shop. To my knowledge through at least sixty years and through all exchanges of ownership it turned out delicious fish and chips. Our parents were not averse to sending down for some for supper – not for dinner. That was not allowed because it would dub my mother a lay-about who was incapable of feeding her own family. Otherwise one went on one's own and cadged a penny for a penn'orth of chips, or if times were hard, a ha'p'orth of crackling which I did in fact prefer. If you were very little you went with your brother, because if your face did not appear above the zinc counter you tended not to get served.

"Here, when are you going to serve my little sister then? She was here ages before that lady."

"What y' want? Penn'orth of chips?"

"No, I've only got a ha'penny – can I have some crackling?"

Then I received a delicious scoopful of greasy bits of batter, with the taste of the fish from which it had fallen. Lionel would add the pepper, salt and vinegar from the battered utensils on the counter and see me half way home before he went on to his own mates and ploys. He was very good to me, with the result that all the older boys in the street treated me with respect whenever I chose to hang round them, and every now and again I felt impelled to indulge in some macho or wild activity to justify his faith in me.

Thinking back on my ha'pence worth of crackling and penn'orths of chips I cringe. At meals I was a good girl and ate all the fat. My mother thought (with many other mothers at the time no doubt) that a 'nice bit of fat' was good for you. Certainly I can well remember delicious stews, which not only were fat in themselves but also were the environment for glorious large dumplings (of which I was very fond). There were also Spotted Dicks, roly-polies, bacon and onion rolies and steak puddings which I adored.

The next place in the street was Draycon's, which was some kind of food warehouse, but their main commodity was bacon. Dozens of flitches of smoked pig hung at the back. They must have prospered because quite early on they took on the large premises opposite our house, rebuilt the front with lovely new brick and installed two enormous green gates which I do not believe I ever saw open. This magnificent spread, uninterrupted by any windows, was much used by all of us, by the boys for Hi-Cockalorum and Up the Wall, and by the girls for all kinds of O' Lairy and other ball games.

The nicest bit of Draycon's though, was their biggest horse, Blossom. Every time he was left unattended in the road outside, he dragged his slide and sallied up the gutter to our shop, where he stepped boldly across the pavement with his front legs and stuck his head in our doorway. At once Mum or myself would be there with a bit of apple or a lump of sugar. The men soon gave up bothering when they discovered his visits were welcome and he did no-one any harm. If they were about to use him they now knew better than to leave him on the road, but would have to back him into the loading bay. Mum and I and Blossom got a lot of pleasure from these visits and I learned how to hold my hand quite flat to avoid his big yellow teeth, and also the plentiful foam he always managed to spray about. Saliva wasn't all he sprayed about sometimes, and what a fascination it was to watch great waterfalls flooding down, hot and steaming into the gutter. Mum would then smack him firmly on the rump and call him a dirty old beast. I thought this rather unfair as when he performed his other function there, she was always pleased. Unquestionably this was on our territory, and the bucket and shovel were fetched pronto.

There was a fair amount of going and coming at Draycon's. This was where gentlemanly Mr Pound worked, but he wore a brown overall and obviously was employed in the warehouse part.

The dark-suited men didn't actually live in our street, but I once (again to my mortification) ran down the street from our front doorstep, where I had been standing in great boredom (I had 'drops' in my eyes at the time – always a torture) waiting for Dad to return to break the monotony. Up the road came this just recognisable male figure with a trilby hat and a case, which I thought was a ditty box, so I rushed down and flung myself up at him to give him a smashing kiss. Alas – it was Mr Draycon. I said "Sorry" and rushed home in tears. The whole family were torn between ridiculing me and feeling demeaned that I should have mistaken this paunchy, dark-suited man with a Homburg and a brief case, with Dad in his paint-stained old trilby and his little wooden ditty box.

Draycon's larger premises had previously been the mineral water and ginger beer factory of Brooks – famous in the town. From inside often came hissings of an enticing kind, and again large wooden crates were flung about and tossed on top of more open lorries, with more handsome feathered carthorses, stamping their feet with impatience, tossing their heads and making their brasses rattle, blowing out their huge nostrils and dribbling and foaming messily at the mouth. It always seemed that every horse wanted to be off in those days, and the only time they were quiet was when the nose bags were hung over their necks. Even then they were not still, because they flung up their heads constantly, I suppose to get the feed out of the corners, and blew lustily through their noses into it so that the chaff flew up into the air all round their ears.

We never quite knew what went on inside Brooks because no-one was ever known to have penetrated its recesses. The great wooden gate-like doors were always closed, but we could hear within the clash of glass bottles, and we could buy their product, but rarely, at the little sweet shops, or get our dads to bring them back from the pubs. These old bottles can now be bought for quite a lot of money at trendy junk shops where they arrive after being dug up in rubbish heaps. Near the base of the neck was a pinched in section and within the bottle was a glass marble. On the bottle being filled under pressure with gaseous liquid, usually ginger beer, the marble was forced upwards against the 'pinch' and held there by the strength of the pressure. It was not easy to open these things – we in the street often tried and usually failed, but most households were armed with a wooden tool like a short circular cup with a stopper in the middle. This was placed over the bottle end, with the stopper above the marble, and then pressed down with considerable strength. Once the slightest movement was made, of course, there was a satisfying hiss, pressure within ceased, the marble dropped to the bottom and the fizzy fizzed out.

If bottles were not smashed more often, to obtain the marbles, it was because better ones could be obtained at about 10 a penny, which you could get back on a couple of returned bottles. In any case the swapping value of a green glass ginger beer marble was low. Furthermore, we did not much smash things in those days – conspicuous consumption had not been invented, at least not down our way, and conspicuous waste was frowned on. Sometimes a man would come out and drop us a few of the glass stoppers from his pocket, but not often. I think a pretty close watch was kept on them.

Next to Grandma's was an identical cottage, then another cemented cottage, then the entry to Payne Roger's Stabling. Here I spent a fair amount of time in the hay loft wriggling around, hiding under the hay, and dropping sticks down through the cracks in the flooring. Fortunately no boys were ever allowed in here for fear of the harm they could do, especially if they had a stolen box of matches. I was privileged as a friend of Alice Picknell whose grandad (old man Downe) was in charge of the horses. I wasn't supposed to play with her, my mum said, and indeed I didn't like her very much, though she did point out to me once that I had nipples and that they would grow one day, as hers were already doing she said, though I could not see they were any different. It was an alarming prospect and I didn't want to know. On the other hand I appreciated the warmth of the stables on a wet day, and it was near enough to home to be able to hear my mother if she called for me.

Up we go next door to the sweet shop that the street nippers patronised. It was incredibly small, incredibly greyish-brown. You went down one shallow step and were in a space in which no more than three customers could stand at a time. An overhead bell on a spring clanged and Miss Cowper came in from her kitchen. She was small and grey-brown like the shop, but I cannot remember anything good or bad about her. She was a neutral person. The shop was always referred to by the women of the street as 'the little general shop'. Indeed there were various packets of food about, not much of anything, a bit of custard powder, rice, tea, sugar, and a few vegetables like potatoes and onions, but of course no tins of anything. Canning had not arrived in England yet, though I expect sardines and salmon happened along very soon. Miss Cowper also had some large jars of piccalilli and occasionally I was sent across with a small basin and a threepenny bit to fetch some.

The sweets were the thing though – of course only the cheapest. You could spend farthings here with impunity and a halfpenny was probably the most common coin. There were a few jars of jellies, fruit drops, acid drops and paregoric sweets. These were my pride and joy, both because I liked them, and because each translucent brick-coloured brick shape was emblazoned with a letter H in relief. These sweets were made somewhere at the top of the town by a small family firm called Holman and, would you believe it, my mum's name was Carrie Holman Bastien, having been named after Mrs Holman.

There were hundreds of little shops like Miss Cowper's, although they did not all sell piccalilli. They made a small living for their owners, and filled an important place in their neighbourhoods. No supermarkets in those days.

They were all almost identical, specialising in the cheapest kind of sweets, which were attractive to children. Pride of place perhaps should go to all the derivatives of liquorice, the most expensive being Pontefract cakes, chewy and full of flavour. Each had a picture of the Pontefract tower stamped in, and were really too expensive for the kids. There were everlasting strips, which I have written about elsewhere, liquorice shoe laces, liquorice pipes which to add realism had a few red hundreds and thousands fixed to the bowl. Then there were tubes inserted in the corner of triangular packets to suck up the sherbet, or lemonade powder, inside. Sometimes the sherbet dabs as they were called, had instead a small dab of toffee on a stick in the corner, which when well sucked carried a good flavour of liquorice and toffee to the mouth. Sherbet and lemonade powder were sold by the penn'orth and with them you could make your own refreshing drink. If you were rich and had bought both powders, the resulting lemonade fizzed satisfactorily. If you were poor you just stuck your finger in and sucked. There were of course other novelties, but not so many as now when you can buy flying saucers etc. Not strictly sweets were tiger-nuts, dried, shrivelled up pieces of (possibly) some root. They had to be spat out after being chewed, especially as about every fourth piece was rancid. The other non-sweet chew was called locust beans, a kind of dark shiny pod with hard seeds inside. Also to be spat out.

The most wonderful sweetmeat I ever had was a halfpenny bar, a very thin slab of hard sugar with exciting stripes in many colours. I adored these, and when the box was empty I implored Miss Cowper to lay in some more. She never did, and if you one day come across a very old lady peering into a sweet shop window and turning things over, you will know it is me, still in search of some hanky panky bars.

Many useful medicines would be hanging on cards on the wall. I remember Siedlitz Powders (for headaches?), Glauber Salts, Epsom Salts, Pink Pills for Pale People, Iron Jeloids, and most important for screaming baby – Gripe Water.

After Miss Cowper's sweet shop there followed another flight of stairs opening straight up from the street, then two somewhat larger houses, with areas or 'airies', which were basement rooms. One of these deserves special mention because, although we are now in a somewhat grey area in which not a lot happened, in the second of these houses lived the Sellens family, related to the Thunders of newspaper fame, and among them young Siddy – the only sweetheart I ever had at that period. I was friendly with all the other boys, because I was Lionel's sister, but Siddy was all my own. It was a brief affair. It is possible that it only lasted two days and I cannot remember Siddy playing out either before or after it. All my fault no doubt. I could write, so maybe I was six, and I asked him if he would be my sweetheart. He agreed readily enough, probably having no idea what it was all about – nor had I. We walked out of the street, along Devonshire Road, turned left over the railway line and half way along Priory Avenue, where I decided we should set up house. There was a high comfortable bank and not much traffic and I knew the district because it was almost at my dad's allotment. I believe I wanted to take Siddy up there, but he felt a bit lost when brought face to face with a black earth path which went up the steps and right up through to Bohemia. Anyway, we sat in the sun and talked, mainly about whether picking dandelions really did make you pee in the bed. I then decided it was time to pursue the marriage so I said (having an old rag doll with me) that we now had a baby and I had to feed it. I was just sitting there with my dress pulled aside, and quite honestly feeling a little bit bored by now, when Dad came down from the allotment and suggested it was a bit late for dinner and we'd better be getting along. We ran on, and when I left Siddy at the top of the street I hissed at him that I would write to him and fix our next meeting. That evening I wrote the only love-letter for very many years, folded it small, wrote S. Sellens on the front and, when it was getting dark, ran up the street and put it under his door-mat. He never met me the next day and never wrote back. I did investigate the doormat later, but the note was gone. I rarely thought about 'my sweetheart' after that, but I didn't much like the way his big sister Queenie looked at me as she swept past. A fine romance.

After the Sellens' there came a strange courtyard sideways on and open to the street, with a glass roof and a house door leading sideways out of it. I always found this a most intriguing and mysterious house and was chased out of the courtyard very gently on several occasions. We thought someone very odd must live there, a witch, a criminal or a German spy – according to the age we were.

The next shop was at some time or other an outcrop or replacement to the Thunder newspaper business. This was very convenient as the station was less than a quarter of a mile away.

If you crossed the road at the top you found yourself facing a curved set of steps which led to a permanently closed door. This was again one of our chosen squatting grounds. We were told it was a small Temperance Hotel, near enough to the station to make it a suitable overnight stay for commercial travellers and the like. We were never disturbed there, but sat and gossiped and played with our dolls in peace. At the top of the street the hill was just sufficient to provide scooter and hoop impetus, and for the dozens of makeshift cars we made and smashed up during the year. Old pram wheels were most precious and at desperate times were a form of currency. The main item, after the wheels, was an old box to fix them to. Sometimes these became really ingenious, with the front wheels fixed to a board which was controlled by a rope at each side.

Next to the Temperance Hotel came three little houses, urban cottages of the usual type, two up and two down with the front room opening straight on to the pavement, and a small garden at the back. In one of these lived the twins with rosy cheeks which they inherited from their rather robust mum – otherwise one was tall and blond and named Dora and the other short and brunette and named Jenny. For some reason during part of our elementary school career they thought it smart to call themselves Dotta and Jetta, so that is what they became. Jetta followed in the footsteps of big sister Helen (who married a Canadian in the first world war). She hung around the pubs a bit in the second world war, didn't actually win a husband, but had a bouncing son. Rather a let-down because the twins appeared to think rather highly of themselves, and rather lowly of the rest of the street. Their father was a little red-faced bouncing man, and sharp as a ferret. For many years I was worried by the little sign on his door which read, 'Fred Rolfe – Blind Maker'. I thought he got about very well with no sight, and could not help wondering what he made. My mum, always outspoken, thought he was a 'cocky little devil', but when we discovered he had befriended the hermit in Ecclesbourne and settled his affairs when he was found dead, all was forgiven. I walked to school with the twins and home again every day, but we never had much in common.

Coming on down this western side of the street we encountered a long wall covered with posters in various states of decrepitude, assisted of course by us, but we enjoyed the hanging of them, which was done with some skill – they always fell into place exactly, even when they consisted of four pieces. Behind this wall, which was the boundary of the gardens of Havelock Road, there was nothing of interest to report according to the best climbers of the street, who went to reconnoitre. So with a little repetition of identical cottages we came to the Fire Station. This was important in more ways than one and contained the fire engine and all the hoses and necessary appendages, with some stored across the road in a lock-up shop.

The cottage next door to it was occupied, suitably enough, by Mrs Crosskey who held the keys of the Fire Station. Her son helped out, and when he left school he was put on the railway as an apprentice and soon rose to be head porter. (This was very handy later in the second world war because the town was closed to incomers in case of invasion. My dad was retained because of his connection with the building trade, and my sister, Muriel, because she was connected with catering. Her most exciting and sad job was feeding soldiers on the pier when they had come across in the notorious and bitter retreat in the little ships. But I could visit my family any time I liked, as I was nodded through by the head porter.) I shall have more to say on the subject of fires later.

Next came a rather strange mews. You went along a closed wooden passage, up some steps and on to a wooden balcony, out of which opened the two or three rooms where the Bean boys lived. The eldest boy, named Major, was the same age as Lionel, so we hung about with the Beans. Their kitchen and living room opened straight on to the balcony – I never discovered where the bedrooms, if any, were situated. Mrs Bean was judged as usual by my mother as a thoroughly good woman, a lady. She had little time to linger and gossip and there was the usual scornful talk about single parents, though the boys' father had actually been killed early in the war. She was seen about in a sacking apron and a man's cap and spent her days cleaning other people's homes, but managed to bring up three boys, and not too badly. Major was a law-abiding boy, Fred the rough and tough one, and Dickie the baby. There was a 'rift in the lute' for a while when Major and Lionel each sent away for a free gift of a small folio of all the planes in the war. Major got his within a week, Lionel had to wait over a month. You see what a name can do. It was not long until I could recognise all the allied planes by sight or by the sound of their engines. I knew of the Bristol Fighter, the Sopwith and the Sopwith Pup, the sea planes and, nearest to my heart, the flying boat. I suppose I admired the shape and it broke my heart when it was scrapped.

About half way up the street, where the slope started, and opposite the fire engine's headquarters, was a covered space which was of importance to all of us great and small. It ran under the living rooms of Mrs Dennis. Being so weatherproof it was in almost constant use for something, whether it was passing or more permanent. This was the famous Stone Arch. The ground was dusty and stony, but dry. It was permanently occupied by an old wagon, never moved, which served as a fort, a home or a prison, but no-one laid claim to its ownership, so there it stood for years. One important job it did was to give us all the ability to balance. The two shafts stretched from cart to ground and formed a perfect, sloping, practising ground for circus skills

*Illustration 4 - The Fire Station*

such as tight rope walking. This covered section opened into a big open space, which contained the back doors of the Station Road houses and those of the few cottages in Middle Street. We might be 'ticked off' for playing in this sector as it was more or less part of the business that rented this space. The front arch was adjoined to the big space that held the accoutrements of the fire brigade and earlier had stabled their horses as well.

On the opposite side of the street was the exciting bit, the fire engine itself, various hoses and rows of beautifully polished brass helmets. On the alarm the horses came galloping up the road and were harnessed with some difficulty because of the clanging of the bell and the general excitement. Then they went charging off to whatever was the site of the fire. Information was always left behind for late-comers, so that they could follow and enjoy it all. We as usual were strategically placed to be near the preparations, but being friendly with some of the firemen we had early knowledge and often got there before the engine. What a time we had – what was someone else's ruin was our delight. I may here refer to the famous burning of Hastings Pier, but that was not until 1917, by which time fire-fighting, like everything else, had improved.

Back to the Stone Arch. The most important renter of workshop premises here was my father who was a sign writer. We had a large workshop at the top of some broken slate steps. I am surprised that no-one broke their necks using them, but they didn't. It was lit by very dusty windows and, half way down, by large centrally-opened double doors to admit really big stuff in and out. None of us ever fell out – which was as well as it was about 16 feet high above the ground. At the end was a small section shut off which was obviously intended as an office, but was really cluttered with pots of paint, brushes old and new, and a few drawings of layouts for signs and shop fronts. I spent many happy hours in this workshop, making dolls' furniture, which fell to pieces as soon as it was finished, drawing, cleaning brushes and stirring distemper and wallpaper paste. My brother seemed to be a bit less interested in it all. Dad never set out to teach us anything consistently, but if a job cropped up he would show us what to do and leave us to it. Have you ever tried to make a bucketful of wallpaper paste given a bag of flour and a kettle full of boiling water? Well don't – there is a point at which it becomes sticky and if you don't hit the exact moment it will not turn.

One of the big, literally big, perks of my interest in the decorative angle of our work, was the passing on to me of out-of-date wallpaper samples. These were truly enormous bound books, too heavy by far for me to lift when little. They only appeared about every second year and must have been very expensive to produce. The amazing designs, colours and textures were a God-given possession for a child interested in such things. They were also useful – the teacher always scrounged a few dozen sheets to cover exercise books and for other incidental purposes. I remember being bowled over by the beauty of those in a smaller book by Shand Kydd, which I thought a strange name for a firm of paper makers, but which cropped up again in accounts of Princess Diana, who was related to the family. The papers were so beautiful that, as my Mum said, "Class will breed class."

About my tenth year fashion in house decorating changed and instead of simply hanging the paper on the wall one had panels of the

*Illustration 5 - Perce Knights in his front workshop*

chosen pattern occupying the centre, with a surround of plain paper, as well as the old frieze which the smart always had. This made decorating a room more interesting and also more expensive. Indeed there were occasions when Dad's enthusiasm for a layout was at the expense of the completion of payment. The next step was to put a different paper on different walls. Often the results were horrible, though its proponents claimed science on their side. You could alter the dimensions of a room by your use of colour. If you wanted to push back the walls of a narrow room you would put soft pale colours (blue, mauve) on the long walls, and more strident ones to bring the short walls into focus. It did not always work.

One useful thing I always wanted to do in Dad's workshop, but was never allowed, was to sweep up. The dust just accumulated on the floor, but the air was clear as behoves a paint shop.

It seems it is going to take a long time to get out of this street, and indeed it did, only partially for me when I went to college at eighteen, and only completely when Hitler unloaded one of his bombers casually above us on its way back over the Channel.

It was a stray German bomb, which fell just outside Dad's workshop and shook the house to a state of instability. He was most indignant, as he was on the roof at the time tenderly nursing the tomatoes (which he grew there) and the ripening fruit was shaken off the plants. Also a box of matches he had in his pocket burst into flames and burnt his trousers.

# Street Activities

**Street Games**

Games in the street were much as playground games are now, with the addition of many a forgotten or forbidden extra. Largely there were many variations involving chasing, tagging and running madly in all directions. We called it Tegga in our town and the chaser was 'he'. This was first arrived at by one of many 'counting out' rhymes such as:

> "Up upon the mantelpiece
> You will find a ball of grease
> Shining like a threepenny piece,
> And out goes she."

Or:

> "Eeny, meeny, miny, mo,
> Catch a nigger by his toe.
> If he hollers let him go,
> And out goes she."

It was easy to break into straight forward Tegga at this point, but democracy might decide to play 'off ground' Tegga, and there were plenty of drain covers, fire hydrant covers, and small walls on which you were safe, especially if you called "Feignites" with fingers crossed. When we discovered that the odd Londoner would shout "Cave" we would not recognise it, thinking it foreign and pretentious. We were a really snotty lot, looking down particularly on London children, some of whom were sent down to avoid the Zeppelins. A particularly awkward game was Touch Tegga where the new 'he' had to run holding the place he was touched. A lot of mirth was engendered if you managed to catch him on the bottom – but better still if you could catch his leg, or, gloriously, his foot.

The girls, of course, joined in the usual fracas but specialised in round games, singing games and ball games. If you got hold of an old tennis ball you were made. Endless variations of Up the Wall were played, like clapping once before you caught it, then twice and so on. Similarly with bouncing a ball on the pavement – keeping going up to a hundred, turning round between bounces, cocking your leg over when bouncing (doing it outside-inward was easy enough, the reverse far more difficult as you lost sight of the ball for a second). There was a chant of:

> "One, two, three alairy.
> I spy Mrs McClairy
> Sitting in the pompalairy
> With her daughter Mary."

There were communal games galore, like Queenie, Queenie who's got the Ball? where Queenie's face is against the wall as she throws the ball behind her to the assembled attackers. If she succeeds in guessing correctly, the ball-holder becomes Queenie. In another version, Queenie has her eyes shut while the opponents move forward trying not to be spotted when she opens her eyes.

Singing ring games never dulled, one wonders why not. In and Out the Dusky Bluebells is one such game, with the leading player twining in and out of the archways made by the others.

> "Take a little dance and a hop in the corner,
> Take a little dance and a hop with me,
> Take a little dance and a hop in the corner,
> Hi, tiddly, um tum tay."

There were many other versions of this, all with 'archways' and choosing the next favourite in. A more exciting one was:

> "The farmer's in his den,
> The farmer's in his den,
> Ee-eye-en-geeoh!
> The farmer's in his den."

Following verses tell how he wants a wife, who wants a child, who wants a nurse, who wants a dog. By this time there are five chosen characters in the centre and the crisis approaches as:

> "We all beat the dog,
> We all beat the dog,
> Ee-eye-en-geeoh!
> We all beat the dog."

A more pacific version was "we all pat the dog". The dog emerged at the end proudly battered. Another one involved a chase at the end:

> "Who's that walking round my farmyard?
> Only little Bobbie Bingle.
> Don't you steal any of my fat pigs,
> Or else I'll make you tingle.
> I stole one last night, I'll steal one again.
> So come along little Bobby Bingle."

And the predator snatches a member of the circle and tears madly away pursued by the farmer.

Girls were also energetically into skipping, which oddly enough the boys seemed incapable of, though very apt to run into your rope and mess it up. I never saw a rope with handles, ever. We knew they existed, but again they were a sign of decadence. As a matter of fact, a plain rope was the most useful anyway. Anyone who could get hold of a length of suitable rope was popular, and here I was able to triumph. There was straight skipping, and also a trick called Bumps, where you had to pass the rope under your feet twice for each skip. There I failed miserably. A long rope with a turner at each end offered more variations for a number of chants, the simplest of which was:

> "All in together girls,
> This frosty weather girls."

Here one entered one at a time, or all together. There was skipping with two long ropes one after the other. I was really good at this one. I am glad to say that we did not forget the tinies, but gave them a turn at Jump the Snake and Jump the Swinging Rope to introduce them to the skipping convention.

May I push in here a reference to something that was best done with a short junior? Two girls held hands facing each other and sang:

> "Draw a bucket of water,
> For my lady's daughter.
> One in a bush, two in a bush,
> Let the young lady come under."

Whereupon the youngster took her place in the cage of the senior girls' arms. They then swung their arms over her head so that they were crossed. At the call of "Under", a quick move caused the child to turn an aided somersault. If arms were swung over in the wrong order, there could be chaos.

While all this was going on the boys might be playing Hi Cockalorum, a sometimes dangerous game which no girl joined in. Two teams of boys were formed. One team placed their largest and strongest boy in front, with his head between his arms, and his hands resting on the wall. The rest followed, leap-frogging one after the other, each holding tightly round the waist of the one in front, thus making a long back, like a caterpillar. The second team, sending its best leap-frogger first, had to land as near the head of the 'caterpillar' as possible. The rest followed in order of achievement. When, and if, all were mounted they bounced up and down shouting "Hi Cockalorum jig, jig, jig," till the caterpillar team collapsed, or not, which was almost never. It was a game which needed great strength, agility and speed.

The boys also hurtled through the streets with their hoops made of iron, with skidooks to drive them. They made a hideous noise, because the hoops had been lying neglected in back yards through the summer and had collected a good deal of rust. Yes, the girls also had hoops, decent, gentle, quiet wooden ones, which were propelled by a short stick. All you could do was pat them along, or take them to the top of the street and bowl them off. Every street in Hastings was a hill, slighter or greater. One could, of course, skip in the wooden hoops, but only one way.

A very useful winter toy was a winter warmer. You made this from an old cocoa tin with a hole pierced in the base and the lid, with a strong cord threaded through. Inside was a crumpled piece of old rag which had been soaked in paraffin. This was lit, the lid replaced, and the whole thing whirled in the air to keep it alight. I was even given one to keep in my muff at the age of three, but of course, deprived of air, it went out. Nowadays people would be aghast at such a dangerous occupation, but I never heard of anyone getting burned. When I was older I became very popular because I could always nip in and soak someone's rag in the drip tray of our oil tank.

We developed the knowledge of the effect of spinning something in the air. We made bull-roarers with the aid of two holes in a circle of cardboard threaded with a double string, which produced something that looked and sounded like a miniature chain-saw. We could also mix our own colours if we crayoned our cardboard.

Another universal, seasonal game was, of course, Conkers. There was first the intense joy of finding them, and Alexandra Park was a good place. Unfortunately it often involved hurling sticks at them on the trees, if the 'Parkee' wasn't there. We then grovelled on the ground, choosing the most likely set of prickles to break open. There inside were these shiny, brown nuts, so that even the least aesthetic of us forgot for the moment that we were only going to smash them up. You must know that one bored a hole through a nut (and sometimes one's hand), threaded a strong string with a large knot in the end through the hole, and let battle commence. Tragedy struck if your conker was ever split at the first blow. It was sure to be shattered on the second. You kept careful account of your triumphs saying "Mine's a fiver", or "Mine's a three-er". You might not believe it, but I once owned a niner. Alas, they dried up and wrinkled and lost their shine eventually. Of course there were tricks of the trade, all employed by the wily ones. Some put them in their mums' ovens when the dinner had finished cooking. There was much discussion as to how hot the oven should be and how long the conkers should bake. Another ploy was to soak them in vinegar all night. I doubt if any of this made any difference, but it kept us occupied. You could also tease the girls with the prickly cases, or give them your leftovers to make a necklace.

One of the most ancient of games still played was Five Stones, known to us as Gobs and Bonkers. It would take too long to explore this in all its elaboration. Being a seaside town we were never without stones of all shapes, but experts thought them too slippery. Somewhere along the line it occurred to someone to make money by manufacturing them out of metal, with projections which would make them easier to catch and retain. I never saw any in use.

A game which required little – and free – apparatus, but a good deal of skill was Tip-Cat. One placed on the ground a fairly robust and cylindrical stick (a small log), placed a second stick across with one end elevated, put another stick (or a stone) at the end, and hit the loose end hard so that the opposite object was thrown in the air. Then one had to hit the flying object as far as possible. Actually, because we never asked for trouble, we used a stick for the cat, rather than a stone.

So you see we were called upon to use much inventiveness in our games, as well as a great deal of craft in finding, borrowing or otherwise annexing the tools of the trade. And we were spared the obtrusive colours, fragility and general unsuitability of today's costly plastic baubles.

## Fag Cards

An integral part of a child's possessions and aspirations were the cards given away in every packet of cigarettes – which had just become a universal habit when I was very small – ousting the tobacco pipe with all young people and many of the older ones. Even ladies smoked (of course the smart set had done so for some time) and very occasionally they were seen to do so in the street. Such females were then thought to be dead common, bad lots, no better than they should be.

However, we all collected the cards, played with them, and swapped them. We accosted every passer by with "Got any fag cards, Mister?" and were received mostly kindly even if they had none to give – though I fancy anyone passing along small streets where children played must have suffered continual irritation. If the asker was seen to be in luck, everyone flocked round to see what it was and offers of swaps were given and received, with much argument and bargaining. If it was a card that might fill a gap in a nearly completed set, generous offers of two, three, four or more swaps were made, and the canny possessor of the valued card, working on her knowledge of the market and the generosity of the buyer knew just how far she could push the price up. Many cards were issued in sets of twenty-five, and there were some of fifty. Occasionally, having completed a set, one learned that the cigarette firm had decided to issue a second set of the same subject. That was annoying because boredom set in, and one's sense of achievement was dulled.

Most cards were the same size. You will be familiar with them because sets are seen for sale in antique and junk shops – the fruits of some old person's lifelong pursuit of completion. Sometimes they are fitted in albums, looking at you through little windows. These albums you could send away for, for the cost of the postage. Nowadays sets are also laid out in frames. Many are so pristine that I fancy some are reprinted for the antique trade, in the same way that advertising pictures of years ago are re-printed. Some, far fewer, were double size cards, which were, of course, prized, but not much collected because they were not common. I fancy the size of the conventional card was to fit a packet of five fags – a usual way of buying

*Illustration 6 - Fag cards*
*Reproduced by kind permission of Imperial Tobacco Ltd.*

them – and the larger ones for tens. More luxurious were those printed on silk that showed things like Flags of all the Nations (in war time), or Garden Flowers, and super-posh ones were actually machine embroidered on silk. I fancy the lucky recipients of these always took them home to their mums, some of whom sewed them on to cushions and antimacassars. (Even though some people still use antimacassars on the backs of their armchairs, probably few of them know from whence the strange word came. Once Macassar Oil was used by smart gents to slick their hair down, and it was from this that these fancy goods were meant to protect the chair backs. Obviously it was the gentlemen who got the armchairs!)

The subjects of the ordinary sets of cards were many and varied, Famous Cricketers (I cannot remember Footballers), Actors and Actresses, Uniforms of the British Army, Animals of the World, Tropical Fish, even Political Cartoons. My firm favourite, however, was Things All Scouts Should Know. I learnt much from these cards, such as never to return by the route you came out on in case your enemy lay in wait for you there, and if you were crossing a desert with no water, you should carry a small pebble in your mouth to keep the saliva running. I also learnt the difference between the spore of a dog, which showed his pad-mark plus the mark of his claws, and a cat or leopard, which having retractable claws, showed no imprint. I found all such information interesting though not really useful in this country. You see how much of the Scout movement originated in the Boer War, and when carried over to the Wolf Cubs, Guides and Brownies it was really ridiculous, though interesting.

We used our cards in yet another Up the Wall game, squatting on our hunkers in the gutter. We never actually sat on the ground in the street as our mothers thought this demeaning. The ploy was to skim, with a backhanded flip, your card against the wall, whence it fell on to the pavement. If the next player's card overlapped the first, he took it and play started again. There were times when we were holding a handful of cards, but not often. A bit like Snap, the game might go on for ever. The trick was always to play with your dirtiest and most dog-eared cards, so you can imagine the state these were in after a time. People would sometimes refuse to play with me because I was mean and mouldy and kept my good cards secret. I was always hoarding and protecting anything that came my way and was notorious for this.

## Marbles

The other currency of the street was, of course, marbles. They came out with the spring when the gutters were completely dry. There were clay marbles which were not always quite spherical, so their trajectory was always doubtful, but they could be used by the more accomplished boys (and girls) to take a trick or two. There were the plain green glass marbles from the necks of ginger beer bottles, an assortment of plain glass ones, and others with twists of colour blown into them. Sizes ranged from alleys to alley taws. The only game we ever played was rolling them along the gutter, attempting to hit, and take, the one ahead. As in fag cards I was not a popular player because if I somehow got hold of a prized specimen I hid it in my pinafore pocket and would not play with it.

We (or I) only had this game of hitting your opponent's marble by rolling it or flipping it in the gutter. Any player whose marble fell from a flip straight down on to his opponent's was loudly applauded. We never played within a ring or with home made numbered bridges, regarding such things as effete. (In later years, marble playing became a 'new' fashion. The champion village was Wivelsfield in Sussex, with our local team, Battle, coming up closely behind. On Good Friday the population assembled on Battle Green for the match, at twelve noon. Afterwards a trugful of marbles was thrown out to be scrambled for, and my own two children joined in, to their father's disgust.)

## More about Horses

I have already mentioned Draycon's horses, including our favourite, Blossom, but it would be hard for this modern generation to understand the effect the horse had on life in the early nineteen hundreds, even in a town. I have mentioned already the avidity with which children in the street pounced on piles of dung almost as soon as they were deposited – they felt useful and valuable in so doing, and earned the gratitude and respect of their parents. I imagine most households had a bucket and shovel parked permanently somewhere at the back, used solely for this free blessing. Also, for children at the age when excrement fascinates, it furnished moments of interest and joy in street life. I am sure everyone goes through this stage, though possibly many would not admit it or like to remember it, but they have a reminder of course with their own children and grandchildren.

(During the second world war, when my mother was evacuated with my sister-in-law and two little girls to a caravan in a field in Oxfordshire, I well remember the pleasure with which the younger child at 18 months, used to crawl round the damp field and anoint herself with cowflops. She was in fact known for years as Little Turdy Ann.)

At any rate we never ceased to delight in the very scale of the horses' performances and watched the dung roll out with sardonic cheers. Perhaps even more spectacular were the steaming waterfalls to which the horses sometimes treated us – such a spate that we took to our heels with shrieks of joy. Yet horses at least used the road, and because of this and the value of their product there was less danger for children than now, in the days of dog poohs which appear unfailingly on the pavements or on any bit of grass where children might wish to play.

But we all loved the horses, the clatter they made, and their dignity and friendliness. We knew which ones to pat, which to feed, which to keep clear of, and which you could safely dare each other to duck under. There were plenty of horses about in our street, usually of the heavy cart-horse variety which used to pull Draycon's delivery vans and the breweries' drays. These were always smart and bright. All brewers were proud of their equipage and entered them in any rural show that was held, and often won.

Besides the horses' friendly presence, was a habit they had in frosty weather of slipping on the tramway rails that ran through the middle of the road. This was particularly common in Queens Road where a sudden short but steep declivity was a trap for horses and cyclists alike. It was a source of great excitement and people came running in from all directions to gaze, to gloat or to help. There was generally a tough type around ready to assist the driver, as it was no mean task getting the poor beast on its feet again. In most cases the shafts had to be removed and the chassis backed away. The horse would be lugged and heaved to its feet amid much panting and eye-rolling. Someone nearly always ran out with an apple or some sugar lumps. In my dreams I never rescued anyone from drowning or put out fires, but I habitually stopped run-away horses, or helped lift up a fallen one.

Another entertainment provided by the horse was a visit to a farrier's. There were several blacksmiths about; one in the Old Town that I used to watch hammering the shoe into shape and size, with the clanging, the spitting of red hot metal, and the hissing and steam when it was plunged into cold water. The best – or worst – moment came when the farrier lifted the horse's leg and held it firmly between his knees, applied the still hot shoe to the horse's hoof, from which clouds of smoke rose in the air, together with a horrible acrid smell. The horse never seemed to mind, or indeed to feel a thing, but I did.

## Visitors to the Street

As well as a very occasional passer-by and the men going to work, there were the services of various regulars. The milkman ranks as the most important. In my early days he came walking with a yoke across his shoulders, bearing a large milk churn at each end. He stood these down with a clang and served his customers from a half pint or pint measure. Housewives had stood a jug out on their front steps with the money underneath, and sometimes a net with beads round it to keep the flies and dust out. Later the yokes were called in and the milkman gratefully received a small cart instead, labelled, curiously enough, Williams, or Davies, or Evans. Why were they always Welsh? The baker also called with a cart made of wicker and a delicious smell of new bread. Sometimes a butcher's boy would come with a wooden trug on his shoulder, bearing an order of meat. This was rare, as a quick run to the butcher's for a pound of sausages or a chop was the way we bought meat, only enough for the time being. There were no fridges and few larders with cold shelves. Finally, amongst the regulars were the postman and the paper man.

Then there were the casuals, who appeared regularly, mainly on a Sunday, but who offered useful items for Sunday tea. One such cried *"Wor-day-criss"*, with a rising note on the second syllable. Fortunately he came early, thus allowing my mother to soak her penn'orth in salted water and pick it over carefully for little snails or dead water-boatmen. It came, for free, usually from Fairlight Glen where the Dripping Well, which never stopped, would keep the stream limpid and pure. Nowadays, alas, it often no longer drips or is polluted with effluence, from cows pastured above it. The big house was said to belong to the two sisters of Clive of India, who were sufficiently well off not to keep cows on their pasturage. The district next to Ore was named after them – Clive Vale. We must have drunk gallons of this water as kids, and the Dripping Well was a tourist item, being pictured on post cards and in guide books. Few ever ventured further down the Glen, which led eventually, through thick woodland and bogs, to the sea, via a fairly high hog's back.

If you didn't like cress for tea you could get fresh boiled shrimps or fresh winkles, all carried in baskets and representing pure gain for the vendor, other of course than the effort needed to gather them. Another cry once a week was *"Pipe-clay"*. It was customary, nay imperative, for Hastings housewives to pipe-clay their front step, or be stigmatised as sluts. Again this was dug at Fairlight where, at the bottom of the cliffs there were a number of large patches of clay, white, blue, and light brown. These were made into blocks and rubbed on the damp step. Many prehistoric remains have been found in the clay. Any methodical system of digs was unfortunately made impossible when the engineers blew up all the landmines embedded in the cliffs after the war.

So much for the itinerant vendors. But a regular fish man pushed his cart round once or twice a week. The fish was fresh but of course exposed to the air. Our man's speciality, or my mum's favourite, were skate wings, very small and costing a penny or twopence according to size. (The body of the skate was eaten, once more, by those strange beings despised by us – Londoners.) These little wings curled up and crackled in the pan and were my favourite fish. You never see them now, I think because of limitations on net sizes, so that young fish can escape.

Other visitors were few. Weekly, an Italian barrel organist played outside our house, and we all enjoyed this very much. A penny was always laid aside on the mantelpiece awaiting his coming. He was cheerful and polite, and fairly silent, but I always wished he had a monkey as organists always had in story books. He once actually played his repertoire through for a second time for me, though it was hard work grinding the handle. There were only three tunes, none recognisable or memorable. Apart from that the only 'music' was provided by a pathetic old couple, she leading a blind old man who gave forth a miserable wail of a song. They never collected much money.

I did once see a genuine nursery-rhyme muffin man, complete with a bell and a tray of muffins on his head. And I did once see what I would like to think was the last dancing bear in England. The poor creature was the height of his master when lugged to his back feet by a collar and chain. He was woeful, shabby and very disappointing in his slow shuffling performance. I must have been very small at this time – it was about 1911 I would guess.

A welcome visitor was the dust-cart. It consisted of a large tank on wheels with holes spread across the back, whence it sprayed drops of water on the road, and on any child who was lucky enough to get within range. It was followed by two sweepers who swept the road clean after it was sprayed. The debris was thus pushed down the drains, where it collected until a drain cleaner with a long scoop scraped it out and carted the stuff away. Later the Council engaged what we called a 'drain-sucker', like a giant vacuum cleaner, to do the job more thoroughly.

# Home and Family

**My Home**

Half way up Middle Street was a shop front and window with nothing much in it, because we sold nothing much. There was a shallow, long step (noticeably unwhitened with pipe-clay due to a strong-minded housewife). The door was half glass and bore the announcement that P.S. Knights lived and worked there. Later a phone number was added.

My dad, Percy Samuel, was, I suspect, the rather spoilt child of a widowed mother, and was fairly young when he lost his own dad, whom we never knew much about, as there were no brothers or sisters to talk about him. He was said to be a French polisher, but on his death certificate he is called a 'decorator'. Way back in the Knights family I think there must have been several generations of men earning their living by the brush. We had one valued document which lived rolled up in a cardboard tube, very difficult to undo, with much twisting, pulling and squeaking, and a final loud pop and a small cloud of French chalk. It commemorated the presentation of a Freemanship of the City of London to Samuel Knights for designing and, I think, cutting the first adhesive postage stamp. I was immensely pleased because I had myself become an engraver and etcher. What happened to it? No-one knows, but I suspect it went off to South Africa with my brother Lionel.

An interesting poster from the walls of Paris during the Franco-Prussia War (rats 10ff, cats 30ff, horse meat 200ff per kilo) disappeared at the same time, and a letter written and signed by Lord Byron the poet. I suppose by the rules of primogeniture Lionel was entitled to them – but he could have asked. After his death his family denied ever having seen them, and they probably finished up in an African dustbin.

Back to Middle Street. This was my home. To the left of the front door was the way into Dad's signwriter's shop, but the short passageway led straight into the kitchen, the only room in the house that we had downstairs. There followed the cement-floored scullery and the sink and tap (cold water, of course). Dad had cleverly annexed the old outside lavatory as a paint shop and made a new one inside the scullery. It was the only toilet under cover in the street.

We did everything in this kitchen: played, worked, cooked and ate with three children, a cat, a dog, a canary, and always a board Dad was working on. For in spite of his numerous workshops, he loved to be with his family, and his easel did take up quite a lot of room. There was one small cupboard for everything, though we later acquired a little safe which stood out in the yard.

At first there was an old-fashioned stove for heating and cooking. It had a big oven on the left, a fire-grate in the middle, and a boiler on the right which we never used. This all had to be black-leaded and polished up at intervals. The mantelpiece at first had a serge cover with bobbles hanging on it, until we persuaded the parents it was not really necessary. On this stood a bust of Dickens in imitation bronze, and on the other side a vaguely romantic, perhaps Art Nouveau, female with 'Nixe' carved into her plinth. She was always known as Mrs Dickens. There was of course the usual clutter of vases and candlesticks and boxes. We always used candles to go to bed with, even after gas was introduced. Under the stairs was the useful old cupboard, for stashing things away, and I claimed ownership of the high shelf, where I kept my few books: Poems of Wordsworth, Mrs Overtheway's Remembrances, Squirrel Nutkin and Alice Through the Looking Glass. The square dining table was used for eating, playing and painting, (with watercolour by us, with oil by Dad).

The scullery was cement-floored, had a shallow butler's sink, cold water and a copper, as well as the lavatory. The copper was big enough for the whole family's wash, sheets and all. There was a grate for the fire underneath it. Washing day meant the whole place was full of steam. About 1918 a hedgehog adopted us. His name was Henry and we gave him the empty grate to hibernate in. Everybody but us turned up their noses and said "Don't you know hedgehogs are full of fleas." I think that is true, but they avoided human beings. Mum was glad to forget the copper, which seemed to make unnecessary work, and do her washing in a big zinc bath. The washing never got boiled again. The last large piece of equipment was a huge iron mangle with wooden rollers, which stood across the doorway between the scullery and the kitchen. It had a magnificent rattle. My Aunt Anne, who liked to think she was a bit psychic, swore she once saw the wheel rotate slowly, as if someone was working it, until the handle came to rest at the bottom of the circuit again. Its other cause for fame is that my brother was messing about with it when the family was out and 'accidentally' put the cat's tail through it.

Upstairs, approached by an enclosed stairway, there were three rooms, the biggest and best at the front above the shop. Not a lot to say, yet, about this room, which we thought rather handsome. If you opened the sash window wide you could step on to the roof of the shop window, a habit not encouraged by Mum who was sure that one day one of us would fall to the street below. It was a favourite sun-spot for both the cat and the dog, both of whom did in fact fall into the street at different times. The cat, of course, landed on its feet, the dog looked first surprised and then crestfallen. This room held the best double bed with wire springs, a table, the only armchair and (glory be) a chiffonier. The usual big cupboard above the stairs was full of clothes. The fire was lit sometimes on Sundays, and for a long period at Christmas. We loved it then, and were on our best behaviour.

On the other side of the little square landing was another double bedroom, cluttered up as usual with a bed, a table, a spare chair or two, a big mahogany chest of drawers, which I still have, and a big double wardrobe. In this was kept not only clothes and the family Bible, but various things we were not supposed to see. It didn't occur to our parents that as soon as they went out together in the evening it was the first place we would make for. In it were our three historical treasures already mentioned, and three large red volumes of the Family Doctor. As well as a lot of words, these contained hundreds of illustrations and plates, some of which opened up layer by layer from the skin downwards. We thought many of these rather rude, and I always went straight to volume two which dealt with procreative organs, but not how they were used.

There was another hanging cupboard which, as well as clothes, contained a weird assortment of articles collected by my dad as a young man. There was a functioning bow with arrows (we were careful with these as we felt sure they were poison tipped). There was a banjo with one broken string, which we tried unsuccessfully to tune. We strummed it anyway. There were strange fishing instruments from the Pacific and two large nacre-lined shells which we sometimes used as doorstops. Many other oddments were there, showing Dad to have been a curious and creative young man, anxious to know about the wide world. Thank goodness the genes have persisted, except in my young sister Muriel.

*Illustration 7 - Kit aged 3 and brother Lionel with Mum, Dad and Grandma Knights.*

*Illustration 8 – Sister Muriel. She had not been born when the family photograph (left) was taken.*

As you see, my parents did go out together some evenings and left no baby-minders – Lionel now being about eleven, and the whole district close-knit. I will always be glad I was the 'middle child'. Lionel seemed too busy dashing about; little Muriel was always too clean and well looked after, being the 'babs' of the family. Until she came along and spoilt the fun by taking his place, my elder brother and I always slept together. When we had been put to bed, the curtains drawn and the candle taken away, there was a short hush. Then, as we turned and wriggled and argued about the bedclothes, the gentle creaks from the looped wire mattress under the feather-bed made us remember that the day was not yet over. Our present situation could still be exploited. 'Tin knitting' we called that mattress, and it was as good as a modern trampoline – though sagging more and more as we got bigger. So now we began to toss up and down, bouncing delightedly while the bed squeaked and groaned and we squeaked and giggled. Eventually we were upon our knees and then on our feet and our heads reached nearer and nearer to the ceiling. When the noise penetrated to the kitchen below, the same litany always came up – "Stop that noise, naughty children. Go to sleep or I'll smack your bottoms."

Mum never did, because we changed to a quieter game, balancing on our shoulders and walking our feet up the wall, till I could imagine I was standing on my head – a feat I was never in fact able to perform. Lionel had four years lead in height and in doing his dags, a fact which, aged four or five, I accepted with admiration and no envy. At last we would both collapse and roll together into the central valley of the mattress, he usually to sleep, and myself to lie in a delicious comatose state.

That leaves one last small pine-clad room which played an unusually large part in the family affairs. As each child got older he or she was given it for their own. An added glory of this room was that there was a bolt inside the door and once inside one felt impregnable. The door opened from my parents' bedroom and there was no other access by stairs, so a previous owner had cut a hole in the floor and fitted a trap-door. Although there was supposed to be a set of steps leaning against the scullery wall, labelled 'Mum's steps', my brother and I soon learned to lower ourselves through, hang on the edge by our fingertips and drop unexpectedly beside my mum who was washing up. She never ceased to emit cries of shock although she was well used to it. Also in the bedroom was a big mahogany chest of drawers, and if any visitor was sleeping there, this was pulled across the trap door. We each had a drawer for personal possessions, and 'Kit's bottom drawer' soon became full of notebooks, pressed flowers, shells, dried seaweed and other treasures. In here was a complete list of all the books I had ever read up until the age of twelve, together with remarks and judgements, and a list of all the English folk dances I had ever learned, with a made up system of notation. This I kept up until the second world war.

Out the back was a small yard, concrete near the house, with a pointless step in two places where there had probably been an outbuilding. The yard ended in a strip of sour black beaten earth in which my sister and I at various times tried to grow things. For instance we were given at school three sunflower seeds, which we had to grow for the war effort, to make margarine. Mine never appeared again and I suspect neither did anyone else's. Then, occupying the rest of the space was a huge corrugated iron shed, chock-a-block with who knows what. Both sides carried work benches but these were covered with junk and no work could ever have been done there. It had a door into the back alley for the dustmen, and so my bike was kept there, while brother Lionel's was allowed in the house. One day while Lionel was fossicking about, he managed to clear the lid of a large wooden trunk, which had obviously been Dad's as a young man. Amongst other junk were quite a number of damp, dog-eared paper books, similar in appearance to the old Tauchnitz editions. They were all published by The Mechanics' Institute for threepence each for the edification of eager young artisans. I, of course, commandeered these and though some fell apart, and some were so damp they were unreadable, I enjoyed myself for weeks. There was one volume which my mother snatched from me and put on the fire – I later recognised it as a story of some merit about a loose woman, but I forget its name. I read Red Gauntlet and several Scott books and finished up with Mrs Caudell's Curtain Lectures which were supposed to be funny.

Perhaps the more effective find, alas, was a big box of discs, the exact size and weight of a penny. It did not take Lionel long to realise that this opened the way to illicit enjoyment. For several weeks the chocolate machine at Hastings Station was worked every day, until one day I went up on my own. But alas! There was a policeman standing very close to the machine, so I fled. This was the only time I tried to pilfer, uninfluenced by Lionel – one might say though, the whole successful system was set up by him and I tagged along.

## Indoor Occupations

The kitchen was a place of work used not only by my mother, but also by the children for homework and, as if he had not enough workshops, it was also used by my father. As I have said, he liked to be with the family and it was an eye opener to me when I discovered that dads did not normally come home for dinner. Ours always did. Moreover, it was not unusual for us to come home from school and find a fascia spread across the room on the kitchen table, or on the easel. As it was often glass you can imagine how we had to duck under to get to the other side of the room. But we were well, though not noticeably, trained and never caused an accident. It all seemed so normal.

We, the kids, sat at the table painting (we all had water colour boxes) in our one and only painting book, which was a rather posh affair with alternate pictures of fruit and flowers, and outlines to colour. I can remember one picture which showed a basket of peaches, each with a drop of dew on it, and the pride with which Mum displayed it – "You could touch the dewdrops and wet your fingers." I, alas, was only one of the admirers, but I did have my own De Vere's copybook to practise writing, although in fact I was only allowed to use it once or twice.

The house was warmed, as I have said, by a huge iron cooker. There was a fender in front of it and I remember sitting crouched over it nursing my doll when I looked down to find something horrible was distorting her face, which seemed to be losing its features. It was a wax-faced doll and I was too young to understand what was happening.

I might as well tell you here what happened to the only other doll I ever possessed. It was known as 'Kit's Big Doll' and in truth was nearly as big as a baby. It had a china face, rather beautiful, and was the pride of the whole family. It was dressed in a lovely white pelisse and cape, and had a pram to sleep in. One day a little friend worried and worried me so much to see this famous doll, that I took it out on to our front step where we were sitting. As you may guess, the little friend grabbed it and dropped it with a crash. There were no dolls' hospitals then – so that was the end. A real tragedy.

The kitchen's largest piece of furniture was an ottoman made by my father and upholstered by him. It had an authentic raised, curved end as seen in chaise longues. This object served as a seat for Lionel, Muriel and me at meal times, which kept us out of the way, and on whose wooden side we drummed our heels if the dinner was slow in coming. It was really too high to use at meal times, but there it was. Through the years it served as a bed on many occasions, and after dinner it supported the body of my dad having his 'forty winks' which were sacrosanct. The top, of course, lifted up and no end of stuff was inside, including things from my parents' earlier life. There was half a pair of gloves which Mum had heroically started knitting for her young man, but couldn't manage the fingers. There was a pair of lady's drawers, thick calico and made like two legs joined by a brief seam in the front. Very utilitarian! But Mum assured us they were the genuine article left over from her 'bottom drawer'.

Also in the ottoman, and only taken out when she was looking for something in there, were a duck and a Mr Punch, both stuffed of course. I never went much on the duck and have no idea where it came from, but Mr Punch was highly valued by me, and gloated over from time to time, then replaced in his hiding place. He was actually a beautifully made creature, stuffed tight so he could stand alone if you got the balance right. He wore a knitted suit, half red and half yellow, a wonderful long nose and a bell on his pointed cap. So I hoarded him at this early age, considered then to be mean and miserly, but now I would be called a conservationist.

There was also an old wooden armchair jammed up against the cupboard door, which at one time held the baby tied in with a scarf, and later myself with my bottom on one arm and my feet on the other. It was in this position that I did my reading. Once I was there while there was great excitement because a Zeppelin had lost itself after a raid on London and was sailing slowly in our direction. However, it never came any nearer than Pett, where I believe it came down. While everyone else was flapping and rushing to and fro I remained calm because I was reading Pilgrim's Progress at the time and felt that God would protect me if I hung on to it. It was from the same stance that one day my dad got annoyed because I would not help with the washing up, so he pulled me out and chased me up the stairs, beating my bottom with a hair brush. This was the only time he ever raised a hand to any of us. Fortunately I was more agile than he on our narrow staircase.

I seemed to be useful in many other ways, but always in trouble because I would not join in the household chores. The result was three definite allocated jobs – consistent I see now with my own predilections. First, I was the one who peeled and sliced up the cooked beetroot. Obviously the glorious colour was an attraction, together with the many effects you could achieve by simply cutting concentric circles at different angles. The second one was breaking up the large blocks in which my mother bought her salt. It was amazing how that filled, more than happily, a long winter's afternoon. One could scrape it down to a powder – rather a nondescript occupation but, given the available knife or other implements, one could bore holes in it, as in Gruyere cheese. One could also cut and carve it in enough ways to satisfy the latent sculptor in me. One finished up by rubbing the biggest pieces together in mid-air, which resulted in beautiful showers of salt 'snow', but also a good ticking off for making a mess. My third job concerned paper and was the cutting of newspaper to size and threading it on string to hang in the lavatory. I got a great deal of satisfaction in precise folding and cutting up with a knife, all of which stood me in good stead when dealing with expensive papers in later life. The other paperwork was to cut up smaller pieces and string them and hang them on the paternal bed-post as shaving papers. Shaving was a constant source of interest to us kids, whether it was listening to Dad stropping his cut-throat on the leather strap which occupied the other bed-post, or being chased round the house with a lather-covered brush to evade a much coveted dab on the nose.

Dad later acquired a big old desk in which he could keep his papers. So there was room for nothing else except the birdcage. Canaries gave way to budgerigars, which had only just been adopted in this country and which we thought were miniature parrots.

One exciting day a gas-stove was inaugurated in the scullery. I don't know what occupied the space before that, but with that installed, and the sink and the boiler and the mangle, and with a child or two dropping through the trapdoor above, there was only room for two shelves, one of which was occupied by the knife board and the knife powder. Knives were of steel (and could cut), but rusted if not cared for, so after every dinner they were washed up and then rubbed up and down on the board, which had a little black powder dusted on it. It was a dirty-handed job, but the knives shone.

Every Sunday lunch time Dad sharpened these knives with a butcher's steel, so vigorously over sheets of newspaper that quite a lot of steel filings were produced. By moving the steel about under the newspaper the steel filings could be made to dance – one of Dad's attainments (which were many) that never ceased to delight us.

As I have said, washing day was pretty steamy at first, as the boiler was filled to the brim with sheets, towels and clothes for five people. It was less so when the boiler grate was dedicated to Henry the hedgehog, but our huge zinc bath had to be lugged into the scullery and filled from boiling kettles and saucepans. Now the wet things could be taken straight out of the bath and put through the mangle, which was a great saving of energy because tremendous strength was needed to hand wring large articles as dry as possible.

This zinc bath was, of course, also our bathtub on Friday nights in front of the kitchen fire. First in was Muriel with the clean water, then after added kettlefuls of hot, myself, then my brother Lionel who was considered old enough to bath himself. My parents must have organised night time baths for themselves. All this water, by now cooling and rather scummy, had to be got somehow into the backyard and poured down the drain.

We never had carpets, which were supposed to harbour the dust, but Mum washed the linoleum floors once a week, and swept and wiped them in between. The only aids to housework, at least in our house, were a broom and a dustpan and brush. There was not even a mop. It was a case of getting down on your hands and knees. When I was about eight Dad came triumphantly home with a 'new' invention. This was really good, a development of the old 'dolly' used to bash the clothes about in the wash. But this was a copper cone on a long handle, with a soap container in the middle. This made washing much easier than scrubbing by hand. We never had a washboard. (Sorry, Lonnie Donegan).

Back to the kitchen table. Perched on the ottoman I somehow acquired the art of reading, probably from a trade journal which Dad took fortnightly, called The Signwriter and Decorator. There were always reproductions of different alphabets in it, some of them Gothic –

unreadable, though perhaps cultured! Others were modern derivations of the classic Roman, and it is marvellous what a lot of versions could be based on it. 'Shading' was much sought after – where every letter cast a shadow and gave the impression of being either raised or embossed. I loved these and was able, by using my early common sense, to work out how the shadow would fall.

I certainly wasn't taught to read at school. As I did not start until six I suppose I missed all the mechanical drill of the first year. At any rate I can remember only one reading lesson. Half a dozen or so of us stood round the blackboard on which was hung an oilcloth banner. It had a picture of a bee on it and a large capital B, and we had to say "Bee says ber." This was fixed in my memory because I was standing next to an unfortunate little boy who had mastoids and the smell was terrible.

Meanwhile Dad pursued his work and enjoyed it, with members of the family drawn in to help as necessary. The most frequent job was to help him 'snap a line'. He never ruled a line, but put a marker each side of the board, with a chalked thread stretched between them. Then he 'pinged' the thread, which left a beautiful straight line. This was O.K. if he was working on a coffin plate, but if it was a bigger job, which exceeded his stretch, it needed me to hold the thread, or to snap it. There was always a small lump of chalk in his pocket and a reel of thread at hand.

A coffin plate was a metal plate of simple or more elaborate shape, bearing the name, age, date of birth, date of death and anything else the relatives wished. Often they wanted R.I.P. at the bottom, which made an extra nine-pence for Dad. In posh cases he had to engrave the letters as well as write them. At times when work was not coming very fast, he used to say, "Even the dead won't let you live," and I thought that very witty. Then the plate had to be taken back, which made another job for me. I never refused anything to do with Dad's work. I enjoyed it as much as he did. It was only Mum's boring housework I objected to. I would run up with the plate to the undertakers, which was in Earl Street, or Mann Street, and mount the wooden staircase to the delicious smell of planed wood. There stood all the coffins at various stages of manufacture, some finished which I was allowed to try for size and comfort. I think that if there had ever been one my size I would have thought more solemnly of what it was all about. Then I would tuck curls of wood shavings into my woolly hat and parade in front of the mirror. I had always regretted my hair wouldn't curl.

Perhaps gilding is a process which should be described. In those days we used English gold leaf. (Nowadays it is probably gold paint.) We bought the gold leaf from Olby's in the City. It came in four-inch booklets, one leaf of gold between two pages of tissue. This was not paper-thin, but even thinner, and moved at the slightest breath. To get the leaf out of the book, and to make it ready for use, one cut up small pieces of tissue six inches by four, waxed one side thoroughly by rubbing it with a candle, placed each piece wax side down in the book and the wax picked up the leaf, but left a two inch margin top and bottom for handling purposes. For some jobs the letters were written in gold size, then the leaf applied with a very little pressure from cotton wool. A good deal of filling up of curves etc was done by using the pieces left on the tissue. You can be sure it was most carefully handled because it was so expensive. A second method was to paint in the letters with gold size, then pick up the leaf with a very thin but wide brush. You had a padded board with a handle underneath and collapsible little side screens, so that when the leaf was being used it did not blow away. Dad put the brush across his hair after each manipulation and when asked why, he said it was to 'pick up the fluence'. What really happened, of course, was that he picked up enough natural grease to take up the leaf. The leaf was placed on the chamois pad and cut to the approximate size with a very thin and pliable palette knife. After smoothing with cotton wool no join could be detected. What happened to the bits of waste gold? Well, there wasn't much waste, as you may imagine – just a smudge or two adhering to the tissues. These were screwed up and known as 'skewings' and saved in an old pillow case hanging on the cupboard door. About once a year these were sent back to Olby's, who burnt them and collected the morsel of gold left unmelted. I think they booked this to you year after year, as one day Dad said he was taking Mum to London for the day. They came back with a new wedding ring – it had taken years of skewings, but it all added up.

You can imagine that the house always smelt pleasantly of paint and varnish, with the addition of the paraffin tank. After the paint shop we must have been a great fire risk.

Don't think it was always work, however enjoyable. We tended to burst into song, or whistling, at the drop of a hat. Dad had a small metal whistle pipe, such as is used to play Irish jigs, which he was very skilful at playing. Mum sang hymns. We all practised a 'soft shoe shuffle', but didn't rise to tap dances.

We all went to London for the day, two or three times a year, and crowded in a makeshift lunch at Lyons Corner House (roll and butter and milk with a dash), went to a show in the afternoon, and to a music hall in the evening, catching the midnight train home. My dad was a great musical comedy lover, so we saw 'No, No Nanette' and others, up to the brilliant American importations of 'Oklahoma' and onwards. My mother was very fond of theatrical families and, like a fan these days, was devoted to the Astaires, the Courtneidges and so on.

## Books and Reading

Apart from the damp, dog-eared and torn books which we discovered when illicitly breaking into the old trunk in the 'tin shed', we had no books or bookshelf. These books had obviously been valued and stored by Dad when a young man. He must have had access to a Mechanics' Library, books priced at three pence, but the coming of real work and a family to keep, as usual kept his mind otherwise occupied. I was able to keep several books that were intact, or considered harmless, so I read Ivanhoe, Mrs Caudell's Curtain Lectures and others as previously mentioned.

Our access to books was ensured however by the fact that Lionel's best friend had left school and worked in Salmon's Library along the front. The hiring fees, although low, would have been too much for us, but anyway who wants to pay to read a book when one can take it from a library without signing for it? Indeed a number of these books never went back, but formed the heart of our small collection at home.

## The Knights

There is very little to say about Dad's family – the Knights (with an s). They may have come from East Anglia – but Aunt Bet is the only clue. Dad was an only child whose father died when he was nine, so there are few people who knew his origins, not even cousins and aunts. He lived as a child in St Mary's Terrace and his best and lifelong friend, Arch Burgin, lived opposite in one of the only two houses that turned their backs on the town. Among the few stories about Dad's childhood was one of getting up in an omnibus and insisting on changing his seat because two men in checked work shirts came and sat next to him. I do know he was known as 'Gentleman Knights' when young.

He and Arch formed later the 'West Hill Bonfire Boys' and it was a tradition to fill a barrel with oil-soaked cloth, set light to it at the top of Castle Hill Road near the castle and roll it down the precipitous hill, leaving some mates to redirect it as it stuck on the corner. It was then left to finish up on the beach in front of what is now Woolworths.

Arch Burgin from childhood till death was besotted with the sea, and both boys addressed each other as 'Admiral'. Uncle Arch, as he became known, was later a lighterman on the Thames. One of the highlights of my life was a day spent with my brother on a lighter. They were long boats, quite different from barges, and appeared to specialise in moving things about on the river, and unloading minor cargo on to the quays. Arch's wife, otherwise rather fastidious, boasted that she had never bought a sack of potatoes or a load of coal in her life. Things got left standing on the banks and 'forgotten' till dusk, when they would be conveniently picked up. This kind of purloining went on till recently. Lengths of wood would come sliding under the locked gates of a yard into a path and someone would be there to pick them up. Security was improved time and time again, but I doubt if purloining from the Docks will ever be stopped. The lighters had a foot wide ledge running all round the hull and it was exhilarating as well as dangerous to run boldly round it. Arch used to tie up for a pint on Barking Creek or Bugsby's Reach while we ate the sandwiches our aunt had made us. In his approaching middle age Arch developed an overwhelming desire to become a 'King's (or Queen's) Waterman', a much yearned-after honour. Arch started a campaign to this end, and wrote letters to all and sundry in his favour and got Dad as a reputable business man (and by then a Mason) to write in his support. I found sundry letters to the Lord Lieutenant of Sussex, the Bishop of Woolwich etc. He got nowhere, and I fancy the recipients discovered that Mr Burgin was not the reputable character he drew himself to be. He was, however, an early motorist, and how pleased we were when he came to visit us on his motorbike, with Aunt Ada in the sidecar. After that he had a continuously improving range of vehicles, all of which endeared him to our young hearts.

After the death of her husband, my grandmother moved to a biggish house in St Mary's Terrace. To support herself and her little boy she opened it as a boarding house and the lodgers became friends and, in time, part of the family. One young man was a clarinettist in the local orchestra and his mother, Mrs Soutar, though she lived as far away as Maryport in Cumbria, used to visit every year, long after her son had died. Like all wind players, he succumbed to the demon drink. Mrs Soutar was part of Grandma's efforts to turn me into a lady and many an hour was, to my view, wasted learning to embroider.

Grandma had the foresight to take out official articles of apprenticeship for my father which bound him, from the age of fourteen, for seven years to a decorator and sign writer. When he emerged from this bondage as a fully qualified journeyman, he immediately became what my mother proudly called a 'Master Man', that is he had one or two working for him. It became necessary to move to the centre of the town and to live where there were workshops available. So he came to 14 Middle Street, which had already been converted into a sort of shop, and he rented a cottage on the opposite side of the street for his mother.

My brother Lionel had been born at St Mary's Terrace. The rest of us appeared in Middle Street. The front shop contained paints, easels and all kinds of paraphernalia which Dad would use for small jobs. It was also used as an office. We had an enormous tank in the corner from which we sold paraffin, or 'oil' as it was always called. In front, under the tap, was the drip tray. By the age of seven or eight I was quite capable of dealing with this, measuring the oil in a pint measure and then pouring it through a funnel into whatever container the customer had brought with him, plus a little extra for spillage. The floor round about became impregnated over the years, and we must have been a major fire hazard. Apart from this there were a few rolls of cheap wallpaper, which gradually got sold, and gas mantles. These were of two kinds, upright and inverted, and you had to handle the little boxes very carefully in case the mantle got broken. Careful customers made you open the box to prove it was perfect. 'Upright' were just that, like little beehives, 'inverted' were suspended on their little clay rings, and were not often used. When either was fitted to the gas tap it was set alight with a match and flared up, after which it was a little stronger and you were burning the gas and not the mantle. I gained a reputation as a clever little girl, aged seven, because I was the only person in the class who knew what 'inverted' meant.

The shop window itself never displayed anything but pyramids of paint tins and, for a few weeks in the low season, the coat of arms of the town. This normally stood in the middle of the proscenium arch of the Gaiety Theatre and came in once a year to be repainted and gilded. We also showed their billboards in our shop window. The result of this was two free tickets for the Gaiety every week, no matter what. So I was able to see many good plays and a few bad ones, some tragic, some funny. Donald Wolfit brought his rep. company twice a year, so I became well grounded in straight, though 'hammy', Shakespeare. We saw all the Poetic Plays which became popular at this time and, of course, the comic thrillers such as The Ghost Train. Many musicals were put on, most of which were surprisingly good, as there was a tradition of trying new work out in Hastings before it was taken to London. I remember my mum telling me that the next play was very sad, and she would like to see it, taking Aunt Annie with her. It turned out to be East

Lynn with the famous interpolation of the words "Dead, dead, and never called me Mother," which did not appear in the book but were highly successful in the play. Anyway, Mum used up all her handkerchiefs and those of Aunt Annie as well, and told us what a wonderful play it was. "I really enjoyed it," said she, "I cried all the way through." One musical, called Bubbles, had a little girl blowing bubbles with her nurse, and each bubble burst to display a different playlet. Very ingenious, and of great joy to me because the law dictated that theatre children should receive a certain amount of education. The bubble blower, being about eight or nine, was sent up to the nearest school for morning lessons, which happened to be St Mary's and the youngster was put in my class. What a thrill. She became my best friend for two weeks and this started the theatre bug I have nursed all my life, but without taking any part. What a luxurious life we all led, with a theatre round the corner, and at one time seven cinemas, and all set in beautiful surroundings.

Nothing spectacular ever broke the calm of our lives. Dad worked, had his nightly pint with a collection of cronies, smoked a pipe all the time, the family loved him without saying so, and his wife fitted in with his requirements and adored him. He was a dutiful husband, taking Mum out every Saturday night to a pub that we had to pass in taking Aunt Annie home to the 'top of the town'. From the Market Cross she took a tram up the hill to Clive Vale. We had our pennies and packets of biscuits (no crisps yet) and were well satisfied until the famous and much quoted day outside The Queen Adelaide, when I hurled my penny from the door across the bar shouting "You can keep your mouldy penny," to the astonishment and, indeed, amusement of all the drinkers. I suppose I must have been ten and I was growing up!

When I was about six I was sent across every night to keep Grandma Knights company. Her cottage was small, warm and opened straight on to the pavement. When it rained she put out her darling aspidistra on to the kerb to water it, and to gain the admiration of passers by. It was indeed a magnificent plant, which at one time sported over thirty leaves. These I sometimes had to wipe with a warm, milky rag. I hated that plant. Her tiny kitchen cum scullery was scattered with rag rugs, which I sometimes helped to make. For some reason it always sported a resident cricket.

Many were the attempts to make a lady of me. I was told to walk with my toes turned out at ten to two. Of course I never did. I was warned against striking sparks out of the granite kerbs with my 'Blakeys'. Grandma Knights once said "I knew a little girl with two plaits just like you and when she behaved like a great boy and ran up and down the kerb striking sparks, one flew up and caught fire to her pigtails so she was burned to death." ('Blakeys' were metal studs which you bought on cards, and which were hammered onto the soles of your new shoes to prevent wear on the leather.) Efforts were made, helped by friends, to teach me crochet, knitting, embroidery, how to make pincushions covered with lace and so on.

    Grandma had one book, a very old copy of The Vicar of Wakefield which oddly enough I enjoyed and read through twice. As time went on I was detailed to sleep at her house in case she became ill in the night. I had the front bedroom. There were small trees in the road which threw their shadows, caused by the street lamps, across my window and were always on the move. I was afraid of them at first, but grew to love them. Strangely I cannot remember anything about Grandma's death, although I was so closely involved with her at the time. Whether she was ill or whether she passed peacefully away I cannot say. Afterwards, everything went on as before.

## The Bastiens

My mother with her constant evaluation of other people's respectability, ladylikeness and perfect gentlemanliness, came from a rather poor cottage family 'up Ore', where the town bordered on the country and amenities did not come very thick on the ground. Her family seemed to be part of one rooted up and down from Greenwich to Dartford and further east. They were reputed to be of Huguenot origin; certainly the name makes that a possibility. They believed that the family rightfully owned a whole street of houses in Boulogne and if only someone could find the time and means to go to France and claim it, we would be in the money. A nice thought, but no one ever did. There were times when I was a child that I stood on the Firehills and gazed towards 'our property'. You could, on a clear day, actually see France in the vicinity of Cape Gris Nez.

    There seem to have been a number of aunts and uncles on my mother's side, but I never knew much about them. I can go as far as Henry Peter who was born in 1818 and christened at St. Matthew's Church, Bethnal Green. Eliza Clara Daycock was born in 1817 and christened at St. Alphege's, Greenwich, in Kent. They married in 1842 at Charlton-Old-Church and the second Henry Peter was born in 1846 and christened at St. Alphege's. This Henry Peter must have been my grandfather, and a third Henry Peter was my uncle Harry. They were not very inventive with male names, a little better with females, though there was a fair sprinkling of Elizas, the last dying when I was about ten, leaving Mum a handsome bureau and a tallboy which I still have, and which had to be collected from Charlton. (*Upper* Charlton, my mum insisted).

A Great Aunt Belle found her way to Birmingham where she lived to a ripe and overflowing old age with a wizened little Brummagem husband and a daughter. When I came out of college in 1929 it was the height of the slump, but I was lucky to get a job in Birmingham and my cautious mother fixed me up to stay with Old Belle and Young Belle till I could find digs.

We have a nice little oil painting of Mum's Aunt Eliza. It had a hint of the pug-dog about it, and lo! Old Aunt Belle had a pug-dog. I have also a photo of a little girl reclining on a rug with a pug-dog, and one of a seven year old with a hoop and a sailor jumper, also accompanied by a pug-dog. No wonder in their old age some of the women had a not unpleasant pug-dog look. The photograph I still have shows one of them in old age, curls across the forehead and a massive and perhaps immovable bombazine body. It looks like the lively little girl grown old, but surely a different pug-dog. I only stayed a couple of weeks. They did their best for me, allocating the chilly parlour to do my work in. I never went back to call, much to their relief as a young school teacher was as much an embarrassment to them as they were to me.

In Hastings there was a widow, Mrs Page, and her daughter Ella, and another cousin who married a Mitchell and had a daughter, Bella. We never called on them, nor they on us, but we were on good terms and greeted them when passing.

There was also a legendary uncle (Ted or Ned) who still lived down the estuary, and was a Radical and a tub-thumper, addressing a crowd from a soapbox on the riverside at Gravesend on a Sunday. My mum thought I took after him, which made my unaccountability more or less respectable.

So in my lifetime there was Grandad Henry Peter, who had at some point married my Grandma Mercy and moved down to Hastings, presumably in search of work. The only work I ever knew him do was gardening and odd jobbing. He had apparently no trade, though he is described on his death certificate as carpenter, and I have a photo of him in an apron and a billycock hat, posed with a group of others in and around what seems to have been a garden pavilion they were making. This must have been just below the Ridge, because in the background you can see the Jesuits' College and the pine trees beside it. He was a short, quiet, grey-all-over man with a trimmed moustache. When Mum took us to see Grandma, usually on a

Sunday, he was always working in his quite extensive garden at the back of the cottage. He was like every member of the family, very deaf. I once took it into my head to visit him when he was doing the gardens of a big nursing home in the town. I said "Hello, Grandad," and he said "Hello, my girl," and that was that.

*Illustration 9 – Grandad Bastien (2nd from right) taking a break from work.*

I was never keen to visit Grandma, but it never occurred to me to refuse; Lionel had refused when quite young and Muriel was always pretty close to my mother's side. We walked from the centre of the town over the West Hill, along the Tar Path at the back of Halton, with a view across the Old Town to the sea, and a hedge of hawthorn on the left, the leaves of which we chewed when young and fresh and called it 'bread and cheese'. Do children still do this, and eat sorrel leaves, and suck the juicy white stems of tall grasses near the roots? After the path was finished there was rather a dreary trudge along the road till we reached the Police Station at the corner of Winchelsea Road. Half way up, on the left, was the Bastien's cottage. We were glad to get there after walking uphill for at least four miles – and then we had to get home.

It was a small weatherboard affair, with a little wooden gate and a pocket-handkerchief garden at the front. Inside there was a room with a big, old, coal-burning stove. In the centre was an old wooden table, which just left room for two or three old wooden chairs. On the hob there was always a pot of stewed tea. A door on the left led into a tiny bedroom, and one at the front to a tiny scullery with a cement floor, a shallow butler's sink and, of course, only a cold water tap. An oil lamp stood ready for the evening. Beyond was an extensive garden with a donikin, which contained a large bucket, covered with a plank with a hole to sit on, a smaller bucket full of earth, a small shovel and cut up newspapers on a string. And many nettles and spiders. No window was ever opened, but in the summer the doors were never closed.

*Illustration 10*
*Grandma Bastien (Eliza)*

My Uncle Edward was still, as always, living at home, and for many years I wondered where on earth he slept. In fact there was what looked like a cupboard door, but on opening it you found a shelf just wide enough to make up a bed. I believe something similar can be found in Scotland. This narrow bed was always littered with comics, which were Edward's only reading matter. He was by this time in his twenties, but we regarded him as a kid because of his comics (which we were not allowed) and the fact that he still lived with his mum and dad. Poor Edward. He was a bigger and more uncouth version of Grandad, and very deaf in middle life, with the typical booming voice of the stone deaf.

We were tempted to look down on Edward, because of his comics and the fact that he was so obviously unskilled, uneducated and uneverything. When I was small I did not recognise his shortcomings, but liked him because he knew a lot about nature, some of which he taught me. He tried to persuade me to grasp some nettles, but of course I refused. So he grasped a handful and intoned:

> "Tender handed stroke a nettle,
> It will sting you for your pains.
> Grasp it like a man of mettle,
> And it soft as silk remains."

He was right, and I trusted him, but only showed my new accomplishment when he was near. I did not entirely agree, because I knew I was not made of metal. The whole scene of the two of us sitting by the bottom hedge and gossiping is really deep in my memory

One other happy memory of him was an occasion at Netherfield, where he lived before settling in Hastings. I cannot think how we got there as there were no buses. We probably took the train to Battle and then walked it, complete with pushchair. I must have been about three at the time, and Lionel a wayward seven. The day in the country was lovely, except that Lionel insisted on picking up the movable hen-coop, which contained a hen and five yellow chicks. He decided to move it to a better place, but unfortunately put it down heavily on top of the family – then there were three yellow chicks and two yellow blobs squashed into the mud. My heart bled. It was always bleeding about something small. Edward eased the situation by whispering to us two that he knew where we could see a fox at twilight. As evening drew on and our parents were still nattering, the three of us went up the garden to the edge of the wood and lay silently in the ditch. Sure enough, as the light faded a great red creature came softly along the hedge, while we held our breath, lifted his beautiful red tail, stood and turned his head to stare in our direction. The sight of those shining yellow eyes remained with me for some time. The fox went softly on its way. Whether it saw us or not I do not know, but it must have smelt us. Unfortunately the memory of a naughty boy and two squashed chicks was what my parents nursed – they were very angry, I was only sorrowful, Lionel apparently unperturbed.

Soon after this the old people moved into Hastings and our Sunday visits started. I hated them. We were met by cups of stewed black tea which I could never touch and Grandma would start on her regular performance whereby she demonstrated the fact that she had no feelings in her hands. They were like claws or talons, which she would bang on the edge of the table, chuckling "Look, Kit, no feeling in them." They were cramped up and immovable with arthritis. Though I had to witness this every time I went, I always dreaded it and felt rather sick, and fled into the garden. She was my idea of an old witch – what a contrast to my petite and tidy Grandma Knights.

This brings to mind a tragedy which I discovered on my way to visit Ore. Though it has no real connection it arouses a bitter memory. Mum had set ideas and favourites among most things. For instance the colours she would always go for had to have a rather special name. 'Crushed strawberry' was one, 'eau de nile' another and 'old gold' a third. She was no needlewoman, so money had to be wangled out of her not very adequate housekeeping to have things made for us, unless she could find a friend who liked dressmaking. On this occasion I was to have a dress to last me the winter. Of all the cloth she had to choose from, she insisted on a Black Watch tartan, suitably quiet and unostentatious, the most sombre tartan of them all – black and dark green as I remember, unrelieved by any thread of red or yellow. Of course I also thought this was correct. It was to have a pleated kilt-like skirt and everything went well, even the hated fittings, and the dress looked very elegant hanging in the bedroom. The first time I wore it was a Sunday when we were off to Ore, visiting Grandma Bastien. I must have walked sedately because all the way there, nothing was noticed amiss. The dress was duly admired, and I could not resist a twirl to show how the skirt went out. To everyone's horror it turned out that the edge of every knife pleat was split – sometimes a little way, sometimes almost from waist to hem. No-one could understand it – it was all so mysterious that there was a kind of suspicion in the air that I had done something silly. I did not cry but the world went black and I really felt it must have been my fault. The general consensus eventually, seemed to be that it had been pressed with too hot an iron – and looking back I suspect that the material may well have been cheap and wouldn't stand up to it.

Mum never went back to the dressmaker to complain. It was not in fact wasted because I wore it, but not to school, and I was told not to kick my legs about too much so that they showed through the slits. The next winter the sleeves were cut out and I wore it under my cotton dress as a warm petticoat. This led to further humiliation when I had to undress to assume the livery of a green elf in a Brownie play.

Anyway I was oppressed – as I always seemed to be – by the fact that my mum had spent her scant money on me and it was all wasted. I can't account for the extreme awareness of expense from which I seem to have suffered at an early age. Although we hadn't a lot, I don't think my parents made a point of this, or even discussed it in front of us. Anyway there was always money for Dad's tobacco and beer, but this seemed just and right, and there were pennies for sweets for us at times and we were certainly well fed, but there weren't extras – only necessities. I once heard my mum discussing her family with a friend, and saying, "My Kathleen never asks for anything. She is a funny one, but she will always be able to look after herself."

The Bastien's first son was another Henry Peter – my Uncle Harry. He was altogether a different, taller, handsomer being than his dad. I do not know what he did when young, but when I first became aware of him, as quite a baby, he was already married to Annie Buffard, my Aunt Annie, a girl from the Icklesham district. I have a photograph of myself, aged two or three months, lying complacently on a little sheepskin rug on Aunt Annie's lap, while she gazes fondly down on me through her thick pebble lenses, from under her beautifully curled and coiled blond hair. Harry at this time was in the Army in India, and there are various photographs of this manly figure, in uniform or in fancy dress, with a dark curly quiff and deep-set blue eyes under shaggy black eyebrows. He came home to live with his wife in a terraced house in Clive Vale and I suppose I was three or four at the time. Immediately Annie's house was filled with the delicious smell of sandalwood and other unnamed Indian perfumes. I was enthralled and excited by the smells and by a bead curtain which was hung from ceiling to floor in their passageway. I passed to and fro through this curtain, forwards, backwards, sideways, crawling, hopping – loving the feel of the glass beads as they slid across me slowly or quickly – one strand at a time or the whole lot with a slightly crashing tinkle, and all the time sniffing in the smell of India. I had to get this performance out of my system as soon as I arrived and while the salutations were being made – because of course I was always stopped in case I broke the beads. Still, no one could stop me passing through them circumspectly several times after that, to go to the lavatory, to go up the garden, or to go in the back room for a cup of tea. The smell of India lingered in this house for years and years, gradually getting weaker till it faded from memory, but the beaded curtain hung there till poor Aunt Annie died when I was about thirty.

Harry and Annie had the one daughter, Molly, Nogs or Noggins, the same age as my little sister – so they were mates. Annie was always reputed to be attempting more family, and had her leg pulled mercilessly by my father, in his jocund, sometimes hurtful, way. He also, every time she wore anything mauve, which was frequently, made remarks about 'mauve for hope' – whether this was a saying current at the time, or whether it was his idea of a joke, I don't know. I was often aware of the hurt that his jocose remarks caused to his victims, though he never suspected it.

Uncle Harry seems to have had a pretty good time in India, with all sorts of social events, I suppose to keep the British Tommy on the right lines. He learned nursing as an Army nurse, and when he came home he went to work at the Institution, in other words, the workhouse. He used to bring tears to my eyes when he recounted how an old couple, destitute and without relations, would turn up at the gates and say goodbye to each other, men living in one building and women in another, perhaps never to set eyes on each other again. The casuals (or tramps) had their own building in which they were deloused or bathed, fed a pretty meagre supper, then given a bed for the night. They had to travel a certain distance before another workhouse would take them in. The next morning they had to break stones to

*Illustration 11 - Uncle Harry with wife Annie and daughter Molly*

pay for their entertainment. I suppose the stones were used in road making. The building is still there today, and guess what, is being made into luxury flats!

Uncle Harry was often round our house and Aunt Annie even more frequently, becoming rather spoilt by my dad. Mum never noticed, or didn't care. After tea on a Saturday we all walked Aunt Annie part way home to Clive Vale, calling in at a suitable pub on the way.

The next Bastien was a girl, Jessie, who had an exemplary character and was rather deaf. She trained as a nurse and spent a good time working in East Anglia, eventually marrying Jack Butt, a well-put-on city gent. They took up residence in Ilford, Essex, 'the home of pride, poverty and grand pianos'. It was a suburban, conformist existence which just suited our prim Aunt Jessie, and was handy for the City. Jack was a good sort, who lifted the elbow in a very respectable way. Jessie would be in bed by the time he came home from the Cauliflower, so there was a lot that she missed. One night Uncle Jack came home rather jolly and exuberant, and started to wrestle with the hallstand, which fell on top of him with a crash. Jessie, of course, heard nothing, so Jack, always the gentleman, decided that he would go to bed on the sofa. He was, though, caught out because he had broken his leg. I stayed with them for a bit when I got my first London job on the Isle of Dogs. I was regarded as not quite conformist by my aunt and although their three boys enjoyed my company it became clear that she found me rather odd, so I moved out to West Ham.

*Illustration 12*
*Aunt Jessie Bastien*

*Illustration 13*
*Mum, Carrie Bastien*

My mother, Carrie, was the next in line and she had no ambition to better herself and no accomplishments, other than ogling the choirboys and running away after church. She went into service at the age of thirteen with a little yellow tin trunk containing a few clothes and a copy of Jessica's First Prayer, given by her Sunday School teacher. How and where she met my father I don't know, but they courted for nine years until he was out of his apprenticeship. I imagine that coming from the back of Ore, she was not quite what Dad's mother had expected for her son, because she herself had skills that Mum didn't have. So Mum always treated Grandma Knights with great respect and a very loving relationship developed which worked wonderfully. Every Sunday morning Grandma came across and organised a major baking session to last a week. It was not that Mum couldn't cook, as she fed us well, but she hadn't time for much baking. I was always proud of the way Grandma could peel an apple in one continuous spiral without breaking the strip of peel. I have never been able to do this. My young sister used to help, and became a good cook.

Next in the Bastien family came Edward, the reckling of whom I have already spoken, and last a girl, christened, believe it or not, Mercy Faith Hope Charity Bastien. I was supposed to be like her, because she read books and developed a brain fever at fifteen and died. Hundreds of times when I was a child I listened to the chant, "Get your nose out of that book, or you will go the way of my sister Merce." I'm still here.

So much for the Bastiens.

## Clothes

At first when asked to write about clothes, I thought there was nothing much to say. As their main purpose is to warm and protect, and as most people's money could just about do this, I was never concerned with clothes to flaunt or even to enjoy. However, if I go back far enough I can remember being surprised at the number and type of clothes deemed necessary in babyhood. First, a penny was placed over the child's belly button, and secured, how? No adhesive tape yet. This was to prevent the baby developing a hernia, whatever that was. Then a long length of woollen cloth called a 'binder' was wrapped round and round the child and fastened with tapes. Other clothes – vests, dresses etc came on top of this and I felt so sorry for the little prisoner. I always remembered this when I sang carols – these were obviously the 'swaddling clothes' we sang about. The final effect was obtained by a really long and elaborately embroidered gown which hung down far below the baby. This was the source of some pride and had usually been handed down through a number of generations. At around three or four months, I think, a 'shortening' took place, which marked a serious spot in the baby's growth. The gown was wrapped in scent and mothballs and put away. The occasion was usually only marked by cups of tea and gossip. In future the baby had a bit more room to kick its legs up. Hidden or not, under all this was the inevitable nappy, a large square of towelling, later with a thinner lining used as well. White flags hung on the lines for years after a baby was born. The modern fashion for disposable nappies and less work, seems to have at last outlived its heyday, as every hole in the earth's surface has become filled up with used nappies. Back to the washing machine!

Even little boys were often dressed in frocks or tunics until they were about three. Then 'buster suits' became the vogue, with little pants buttoned to a bodice-like top – very practical in trying to keep the boy dry. I can remember little about older boys' clothes, I visualise quite a lot of jerseys and tweedy jackets. Knickerbockers, and later shorts, were definitely the only wear until a new milestone was reached at about thirteen or fourteen when a boy went into 'long'uns'. An important step upwards. Similar 'rites of passage' awaited girls. When they left school at thirteen or fourteen, it was assumed to get a job, the hem of their skirt was lowered to ankle length and their hair pinned up. A proud moment for them, but one I looked forward to with dread when I was young.

Among small boys one could sometimes come across 'little heroes' in sailor suits, or at least with sailor collars. We thought these little darlings were cissies. The fashion of course was a copy of the Royal Family. Broad brimmed straw sailor hats protected both boys and girls from too much sunlight.

Back to little girls' and ladies' pants. I have already described the separate calico legs which were gathered into a band only at the waist. These had now died out but small girls were still faced with almost insuperable obstacles with buttons, and the shrill shriek of "Mumee, I want to wee-wee" was heard in the land. Then, someone invented, or introduced, elastic to the world, and little girls learned to cope. But like many useful new ideas, it was looked at askance. Would this new stuff constrict your daughter's insides and bring on all sorts of horrors in later life? Of course, convenience won. Girls' dresses were simple. On the whole it was only necessary to have three holes at the top and a good spread at the bottom. Gingham, calico or aeroplane fabric were used by the dressmaker, who would make clothes for almost nothing and be glad of it. I remember standing for what seemed hours while she pinned and altered, pinned and altered, while I fidgeted. On one occasion my mother wanted some 'nun's veiling', whatever that was, to make my prize-day dress. She happily found some, but annoyed the teachers by having it decorated with neat French knots and feather-stitching. Another step-stone in the emancipation of girls came when the 'liberty bodice' was introduced and held sway for many years.

As for grown-ups, the male outfit did not then lend itself to exuberance. My dad always wore the same old paint-stained suit, but had a navy blue one hidden away for funerals. He always wore an old trilby hat. A very poignant moment for me came after his funeral when my elder son looked at this trilby hat on the hall stand and said, "Grandad won't be using that any more, will he? Can I have it for a cowboy hat?"

Blazers were not worn, but men of some substance favoured Norfolk jackets when out of the office, as did my Uncle Jack. Sometimes they sported knickerbockers to finish the picture.

My mother was always neat and tidy and favoured a blouse and skirt. She also had a navy 'coat and skirt' hidden away in the wardrobe for funerals. Cotton house-coats (called 'overalls') were in everyday use. My grandma favoured a black sateen apron, which she coyly laid over her jug when she visited the 'Jug and Bottle' department of the adjacent pub for her lunchtime drink. She never entered the pub itself. Her obeisance to fashion came when she had insisted on buying, at some expense, a widow's peak bonnet adorned with beads and bugles and a wide satin bow.

Hobble skirts were in, but no good if you had to do your own shopping or pursue recalcitrant kids. Gloves and hats were part of the outfit. Some gloves, when worn for effect, went as far as the elbows. There was a long period when straw boaters were worn by women. One day my mum was walking out with her young man, in Wellington Square, when a cat fell from a very high building there. True to form it landed on its feet, carefully spaced round the brim of her boater, which split and then encircled her neck like a collar. The cat was comfortably stretched across Mum's head, but did not stop to apologise. This was her only appearance in the local paper, which finished the story with "…. the lady gave a slight scream." Needless to say this phrase was taken up and used hundreds of times in stories.

Hats went from large over-decorated dishes to the 'cloche' hat of the after-war years, which was considered very fast. Veils were often worn round the edge of big hats, often plain, but coyly sometimes carrying one beauty spot. Hat pins were necessary to pin the large hats to the bun. These were six to ten inches long, very sharp, and very good for fending off unwanted admirers. The blunt head carried many designs: fish, buds, leaves; and modern collectors have accumulated an interesting collection at a reasonable price.

Fashions lasted a long time in those days and there was not the hunger for change and yet conformity, that we feel increasingly now, added to a need to be different.

## Food

Of course the earliest form of food that our species needs is provided for them immediately after birth. I imagine that at the earliest time of which I am writing breast-feeding was done by the very great majority of mothers. Any formulaic mixture of other ingredients would be used if the baby was not progressing satisfactorily. It was not until about the Twenties that some people began to shrink from nature – perhaps the change in the female silhouette to a flat chested, boyish one was something to do with it. Perhaps it was an early, though misguided, sign of female emancipation.

After milk was superseded by some mixed feeding, obviously what the family ate was modified for the baby's consumption. Breakfast though, when I was a small child, always consisted of broken up bread and hot milk with some sugar. In some parts of the country it was known as 'pap'. During the war the first cereal, known as Grape Nuts, appeared, a somewhat granular production to which we added milk. Quite soon after, something almost identical to modern cornflakes appeared – this was called Force. On the packet was the verse:

> "High o'er the fence leaps Sunny Jim,
> Force is the food that raises him."

With a somewhat Uncle-Sam-like figure, with a pigtail at the back, it was the first logo that I can remember. For years after – and still – the flood of breakfast cereals came thick and fast, obviously cheap to make, and selling at great profit. Competition became so great that later, little plastic figures were added as a bribe. The trade still flourishes.

Tinned food began with Pork and Beans, baked beans with a small square of fat pork on the top, which always of course went to the man of the household. Quite soon came condensed milk (always sweetened, so useful to spread on bread and butter if the jam had run out). About the same time appeared Café au Lait – rather like condensed milk flavoured with coffee. This was absolutely gorgeous but did not, alas, live long. Now came the arrival of pineapple, which most people had never heard of, in spite of the fact that it was cosseted and nurtured in the glass houses of the very wealthy to form centrepieces for their table adornment. Quite a controversy waged for some time. Were the squares better than the rings? Which was most economical? And so on. Most fruit, that was grown to perfection in this country, was not tinned at first, though I believe pears followed fairly quickly.

Later came the refrigerator which brought a complete revolution with it. I would be going out of our period if I traced the freezing of single articles through to complete meals, and the wholesale carriage of any and every kind of food by air which we enjoy today. There is a price to pay for this luxury, and I rather think that price is paid by the scant wages of the labourers where it is grown – as also by the loss of agricultural jobs in this country.

## Early Christmases

Christmas when I was a child was a cosy affair – quite different from the blatant festival of today. It began about two weeks before the 25th when the children of the family went scouring the countryside for holly bearing berries, and ivy of which there was always plenty. If we found some berries in a very obvious place we would cut a few branches before someone else did. If it was in a remote or unlikely place we made a mental note to come back later. We depended on the stalls to get a late six pennyworth of mistletoe.

This formed the mainstay of our decorations. We then set about making our paper chains from strips of varicoloured paper bought in small twopenny packets. There was always flour paste about in our house, but we got in rather a mess if the paper was thin. One strip of paper was threaded through another, literally making a chain. It was a great help when the strips were sold with gummed ends, so all you needed was a lot of lick. This kept us kids busy for several weeks. All those fragile chains just had to be hung to save them from destruction. The system was almost universal, from corner to a heavy gas bracket in the centre of the room, from centre back to wall and, if you had any left, from one picture to another. We had no balloons, and when they appeared later they were too precious to put in danger next to holly or gas. That was it – a complete decoration for one or two shillings.

As for a Christmas tree, we saw these in storybooks and regarded them as something you had if you were rich. However, we sometimes cut a fir branch in the woods and it made a fine tree. We had candles which lasted from year to year and they stood in metal holders on the tree. When lighted they were very pretty, but everyone had to be on their toes in case of fire, of which there were frequent little ones.

Then a start was made on the food. Mum and I went to the butchers to choose a nice round of beef to be put in cold storage. In good times there was also half a ham and, most fun, the brawn, which was like nothing sold under that name these days. You bought half a pig's head (sometimes a whole one), dropped it into a large saucepan of boiling water for a while, then the whole family sat round the kitchen table with sharp knives, sliced it up, then cut it all in one-inch cubes. The whole lot was boiled slowly to extract as much jelly from the skin as possible and, if any were available, we added a pig's trotter or two. These were the best times, because the trotters were removed from the saucepan and Lionel and I were allowed to have them for supper. Believe me, if you have not eaten a trotter you haven't lived. After all, in France you can buy a bag of pigs' ears and tails, ready boiled and eaten cold. We filled all available jelly moulds with the cut-up and boiled mixture, and when it was set there were always three layers, at the bottom a layer of meat, then a layer of clear jelly, and a thin covering of fat to finish up.

What about the bird? Christmas was the only day of the year we had a chicken, so it had to be a fine one, and it had to be reasonably priced. In my mind every Christmas Eve was drizzly when Dad and I sallied forth as late as possible, looking for a bargain, which we usually got. The stalls and butchers in Queens Road seemed to have hundreds of carcasses hanging in the rain, with people walking cheerfully up and down eyeing them. This went on till it felt like midnight to me. The other thing we bought as well was a box of tangerines, a new fruit packed in nines in shallow trays, every other one wrapped in foil. We were sure these somehow were superior.

The arrival of tangerines signalled a new method of stocking filling. We still dropped a gilded walnut in the toe, then followed it up with a foil-wrapped orange. Small toys came later. The stockings were hung on the bed-posts with much care and we sang:

> "Hang up the baby's stocking,
> Be sure you don't forget.
> The poor little dimpled darling
> Has never seen Christmas yet.
> I told her all about it,
> She opened her big blue eyes.
> I'm sure she understood me,
> She looked so pretty and wise."

Taking care not to disturb the warm brawn too much, my mother set about the preliminaries for the next day. In the excitement I have forgotten the

Christmas pudding, the mincemeat and the mince pies, all absolute necessities. Nobody we ever heard of bought any of these things. It was a magnum opus doing them for yourselves, but also fun, and it was necessary for all to help. It all went towards a cohesive family. Pounds of sultanas were used, then pounds of currants, which had to be washed and dried – they were usually filthy. Then came the raisins, big and luscious, and they all had to be de-seeded. This was a mucky, sticky job. Apparently seedless raisins had not been produced. Then came the peel – whole half shells of oranges and lemons, mostly still containing a semi-circle of solid sugar, with Mum's eagle eye to see you didn't eat too many. The cutting up of peel was difficult, but our family was famous for its ultra-sharp knives. Last was added a fair amount of suet, some being put aside for the mincemeat, while the rest of the mixture received the flour and whatever else goes in a pudding, which included, surreptitiously, a threepenny piece, or a tiny china doll made for the purpose. Then the mixture had to be boiled in pudding basins covered in greaseproof paper and then in a pudding cloth and tied firmly. Christmas puddings were cooked in the old copper in the scullery (Henry, the hedgehog, being temporarily housed elsewhere). We made three or four puddings. Then they were unwrapped and allowed to get cold. One was put away for a year, the pudding we ate on Christmas Day being one that had been made the previous year. These never deteriorated, they kept perfectly, probably helped by a little something Dad had poured in. I remember we thought my dad was the greatest inventor in the world when he doubled the size of the cloth so that he could tie ears to pull it out of the hot water.

During the first world war, when sugar and fats were scarce, many people started using minced carrot. The result was very pleasant, but of course you could not keep the things made with it because they went bad. Remember the present fashion for carrot cake is only dependant on eating it fresh.

Our cake had been made of the usual goodies and the top decorated with concentric rings of almonds. Mum didn't feel competent to attempt icing, but as we grew to about 13 or 14 we took on the job with varying success. On the top it said 'Happy Xmas', but there were no bought ornaments. We made a frill from crepe paper, which had recently appeared in the shops. The cake was sometimes put in a very slow oven when we got back from church on Christmas Eve, and switched off at dawn. So we never had a cake which sagged in the middle, unlike Aunt Annie's, which were so unpredictable that she would not tell you whether she had made a cake or a pudding. It depended how it turned out.

Christmas was almost the only time you saw nuts in the shops, and in our house a large quantity were consumed. There were the burnt fingers when we roasted chestnuts, someone or other who showed off how many walnuts he could crack with his bare hands, and my father's speciality of using a brazil nut like a candle. Every year we were surprised that it burned as brightly and for so long. I ate a quantity of almonds, because they often had two kernels. One kernel was given to your favourite person and one was kept. The next day, the first person to display his or her kernel had to receive a gift. I usually chose Mum, because she always forgot and had to pay me with a sweet.

On Christmas Eve, from the age of about ten, we were dragged off to Midnight Mass at Holy Trinity. Afterwards we fell into bed, checked the stockings were still there, and slept for a few hours, to get up in the dark cold morning to feel in the stockings again, to eat the orange and any spare sweets we could find in the dark, and try to guess by feel what was in the small (very small) paper parcels.

Various bottles had been saved up for the occasion, and our share was ginger wine or lemonade. A good ginger wine was in fact slightly intoxicating. Any way, we were on a high all day. My Aunt Annie, who was often in the house and was pandered to by Dad, discovered Benedictine and was enchanted. I think half the time she was artificially merry. Even we kids had a taste and nearly choked.

As you may imagine, Christmas Day was spent in gloating over our few gifts, preparing meals, eating them, and washing up. Dad did this while Mum sat in the armchair with earphones on. My mum's troubles were kept at bay because, while we washed up, she stood straight up to listen to the Queen's speech on a crackling crystal set. Or could it have been the King? Anyway, in those early, awesome days when His or Her Majesty seemed right in your own sitting room many people stood at attention for it, and some old soldiers stood at full salute.

Otherwise we played cards, interminable Snap or Driving Jack Out of Town, called by some Beggar My Neighbour. When a bit older we joined in Whist and other games, our favourite being Newmarket. We were allowed to gamble, either with matchsticks or with farthings, which were kept by the dozen in a pot on the mantelpiece. Mum did not much approve of the latter, as being real gambling – you might win (or lose) as much as threepence which was a bit unholy. We played many other childish games, but were mainly occupied in digesting our dinner.

Then came teatime, and I remember that on one occasion, when Dad had bought a box of French Fancies, as well as all the homemade goodies, he gazed at the table and said "This is ridiculous, all this food, and we can't eat it." And then he went out into the surrounding streets to bring in some down-and-outs and tramps. He came back very disgruntled. "There was not a single starving person to be found."

No Christmas would pass without crackers and these were also of crepe paper with a modest little sticker on the front, a paper hat and a riddle inside. They tended to have a resounding crack, and sometimes a flash – rather frightening.

Two or three days before Christmas we had dismantled the double bed in the best bedroom, stored it somewhere standing up against the wall, and lit the fire in the grate. Thus we automatically became members of that class which had not only a dining room, but a parlour as well. I can't describe what a feeling of bliss, of comfort and of familial closeness there was, complete with dog and cat.

So the evening was filled with cards and board games. We had always had Ludo and Snakes and Ladders; now was added a race game, very posh, called Minoru, after the King's horse which had won the Derby that year. This was a splendid affair with lead horses and a green cloth for the race-course and dice of course. In later years this was followed by further games, some of which entailed a great deal of shouting. I remember Pit, which concerned the American Corn Exchange, and many others, none of them thank goodness, as professional or as long drawn out as Monopoly.

About this time a little top or flat-sided spinner came on the market, with instructions on the side which landed uppermost. Soon every child's pocket contained a Put-and-Take spinner.

We sang carols but only spontaneously, and were not worried much by other carol singers, who at least knew their words in those days. Usually two or three of Lionel's teenaged mates had joined us.

Pelmanism had appeared, and brought with it a new belief in the power of the mind. So that, on the suggestion of Monsieur Coué, we kept saying: "Every day, in every way, I am becoming better and better."

Stand your company in a close circle, place one blindfolded person in the middle and all concentrate on the member of the circle who had been chosen to attract him. It was weird to see the central figure sway to and fro, and always land in the arms of the chosen person. Of course, if some one was a bit drunk or giggly it wouldn't work, but otherwise it did. Another trick of concentration we practiced was lifting a man with five fingers. The man sat in an ordinary chair, feet flat on the floor, arms bent at the elbow and lying tight across his thighs. Five people stood by with fingers at the ready. Someone counted slowly while all who had their doubled fingers placed under his knees, elbows and chin, breathed in deeply, and with a sudden expulsion of air, raised the stiffened figure from the chair. It's hard to explain, but it never failed if the players were serious. I have seen a six-foot man raised in this way till his head hit the ceiling.

There were all sorts of other ploys, many of which caused amusement at the expense of the innocent player. Sit on a bottle longitudinally on the floor with one heel resting on the other foot. Pick up a match-box placed on one side of you, and strike a match picked up from the other side. Sounds simple but it is not possible without touching the floor with hands or both feet. Another trick I could actually do was to sit sideways on a kitchen chair which had a safety pin stuck in the furthermost leg (of the chair!) and get it out with my mouth, again without touching the floor or falling over. There were dozens of other games, most of which were inclined to end in mirth at the expense of the player.

Finally back downstairs to see what more of the ham, brawn, cold beef and mince pies we could consume. As you may expect there were times when one or other of us fell out with a bout of indigestion. Christmas slowly faded away, the cold joints got smaller, the double bed was re-assembled and the grate was cleared. Next, hopefully, would come the snow.

## Neighbours

One sometimes gossiped with 'her next door' if you met her in the street, or if you both answered your front door at the same time, and of course when putting the washing out. One never went into another house to talk over a cup of tea. That was left for the ignorant women we sometimes encountered, who had come from the North or the Midlands, and it showed that the work was not getting done. We did not as a rule quarrel or harbour resentment, even if the boys squirted drying sheets with a water pistol. Worse, was the habit of the local birds of dropping ripe mulberries from the spectacular and unusual mulberry tree which, with an equally tempting pear tree, stood in the unused garden of the Havelock Road business premises behind us.

Two sheets and sundry smalls completely filled the small drying space of these little houses. It was a miracle that there was not ill feeling, especially as I used Mrs Apps's yard to enter ours when I was locked out. She kept her dustbin in a useful position, so that even a little girl could climb over the wall and drop the other side. From here it was an easy climb onto the scullery window sill, an arm through the top of the window, which was always open, blind groping to the right until one's hand met the bolt which fastened the door, allowing ingress.

# Outside Activities

## Organisations

I must have been a 'joiner' from a very early age, unlike Muriel who would never join anything. My first experience was as a member of the Band of Hope run by the chapel which the twins, Dotta and Jemma, attended. I could not recognise the big hall we met in as a church, it seemed bare after the Victorian Gothic of Holy Trinity to which I was accustomed. I suppose someone said some prayers on our behalf and we learned to sing 'My drink is water pure from the crystal spring' and 'Let your little light shine'. There was also a rousing hymn sung, it transpired, to the tune which I, many years later, sang as 'Here's to good old whisky – mop it down, mop it down' etc, but we sang:

> "There's a serpent in the glass – dash it down,
> Like a snake among the grass – dash it down."

As I could not imagine anybody deliberately smashing a glass, I thought it meant drink up its contents quickly, rather a contrary lesson from what was intended. The only other thing I learnt was that the shortest verse in the Bible was 'Jesus wept'.

There came the day when an important visitor arrived bearing a bundle of papers. These were 'The Pledge'. We had to sign that we would never touch strong drink. When it came to my turn I refused, which caused a furore and, when asked why, I said "I can keep that pledge today, but when I grow up I might want to drink, and I don't want to break a promise, especially a printed one." Logical child!

The next thing that happened and which closed down the class, was the murmur, or even proclamation, that the benevolent old boy who ran it was too fond of little girls and sat them on his knee and patted their thighs. I wonder how much harm is caused to little children, not by the action, but by the horror shown by the parents and others.

The next lot I joined was a sewing class run by our church visitor at her house. I courted disaster by telling her the doll shapes she had drawn on cloth for us to sew round were too skinny. When stuffed, having been turned outside in, I was right. "You ought to feed your babies better," I said. Little Miss Perky. As a matter of fact I never intended any rudeness, I was just a bit too glib. I only stayed a couple of weeks, but on her bookshelf, into which I was always peering, I saw a 'Crimson Fairy Book', and was enchanted by the illustrations, in black and white, by Charles Robinson, Walter Crane and other famous artists. I asked if I could read it and then if I could borrow it, and took it home. Alas I never went back to the sewing class, neither did the fairytale book. It was a long walk on a dark night.

Next I joined the junior club run by the C.A.W.G. – Christian Alliance for Women and Girls, which was held upstairs along the front towards the pier. My most vivid memories of this were the beginning of the evenings, before the other girls, and the women who ran it, had arrived. There was an open door and an open piano. The trick was to make a thunderstorm by flashing the light on and off, while crashing large chords on the lower keys of the piano. We were never stopped or interfered with. The meetings consisted of talks about the countries the missionary had been into to preach the gospel. We looked at pictures and she taught us a native 'M'bele' song:

> "M'mnya m'bele m'tantu,
> Le missis bombeli the senza,
> Le senza y fili,
> Le missis golily,
> M'unyer m'bele l'tantu."

This was translated as 'One, two, three, Mother caught a flea,' at least more amusing than the Band of Hope hymns. She organised a concert at which we sang this song.

That club closed and next I joined one run by the Y.W.C.A., a very similar set up, but evidently more stable, so when the leader organised a concert it was quite well attended. Again we sang native songs and did a little dance. My best remembrance of the Y.W.C.A. is that on the way there one night I turned over a tray of books in a junk shop and there was The Food of the Gods by H. G. Wells, whom I had met before amongst Lionel's books. It was marked three pence so next day, having cadged three pence from someone, I ran along and bought it and enjoyed it tremendously.

The next organisation I joined was the Brownies and I stayed in it as a Girl Guide, only leaving at 16 when I had to become a Ranger – so boring. I never actually joined myself. Lionel, who was a keen Scout, thought I ought to join and by some trick he went with me and the Bean boys to the door of Trinity School, opened it, pushed me in and held the handle so I could not get out. There I was, stranded. "Oh how nice. Do you want to be a Brownie?" said the Brown Owl. What could I do but say "Yes"?

I did not need to be taken by force after that. There was companionship, room to run about, a uniform and better still we learnt a lot, if we chose to. I could overlook the idiocy of the jingles belonging to each Six. My Dad was highly amused when I was made a gnome and sang:

> "Here we come, the laughing gnomes,
> Helping mothers in their homes."

He didn't go much on me as a home help, but it was better than:

> "Here we are, the little fairies,
> Always singing like canaries."

But I lapped up first aid and became an ace bandager and was able to remember all the right words. I had complete confidence in my own powers. I wonder now what the results would be if I found someone in need of first aid.

Moreover I was fascinated by signalling and soon mopped up semaphore. I could not only send it, but read it if my other half managed to get her flags in the right position. Lionel still encouraged me and with him I learned the Morse code, which was not in the syllabus of such young children. However, when I became a Guide I could use it both with sound (buzzers) and light (flash lamps).

We went on Church Parade about once in six weeks, having first been inspected rigorously. In those days our uniform was a thin cotton dress, cut rather like an elongated shirt with breast pockets and epaulettes. There was a yellow kerchief and a straw hat. Compared to all this, the new Brownies are dressed in the height of fashion.

There were badges to qualify for, triangular ones that were sewn on our sleeves. I think I got quite a few, including an Entertainers' badge (singing, dancing, reciting, ha! ha!), an Authoress' badge, of which I was the only successful claimant, and many others of a more practical nature like Cook, Signaller, Artist, First Aider – you name it, we had it.

All this took place in the old Trinity School, which later became a gigantic secondhand book business, dealing largely with America. It is still there with the trains rushing overhead on a viaduct, as ever. The first troop of Scouts and company of Guides were attached to the chapel in Cambridge Road known, of course, as the First Hastings. We, part of the Trinity Church organisation, were the Second Hastings, but we soon amalgamated. Our headquarters then were the enormous buildings in Priory Street, full of halls, smaller rooms and, better still, cellars.

## School – St Mary in the Castle

Having missed my first year at school through having scarlet fever, I had enjoyed a sort of gap year in the street. I imagine I would have been anti-learning, but whether or not that was the case, learning was not really on offer. The building was as usual the red brick kind of place to dispose of infants, junior boys and junior girls. It was on a very small piece of land, Prospect Place, on the hill overlooking the town and, especially, the cricket ground. The pub at the bottom named it Bedford Hill and the road that ran at right angles to this was the main road of the town, Queens Road, with Police Station and all useful and commercial buildings grouped at the bottom in Middle Street – our street.

There was no room for expansion. There was a pocket-sized playing ground, half covered by the school, and half open to the sky, with a rather dangerous ramp leading down to it and the usual sordid offices. Drill was carried out by the girls here, and the boys' drill was taken on a roof playground. Sometimes they were marched off in twos to a nearby hall of some kind. The infants had just one room to run about in. Any form of sport, as such, was out of the question. Indeed, the object of education at this time was to keep bums on seats, which were always, of course, fixed in position. If there was a room a bit larger than usual it was fitted with a stepped floor. This meant the children at the back could see the teacher, and vice versa. It also meant these rooms became a giant drum of four or five tones. The noise when the whole class moved was unbearable, and there was always a young upstart who preferred stamping his feet to intoning poetry and, particularly, tables. Fortunately the one thing that will keep any class quiet is a story, so many hundreds of stories poured out of the mouths of teachers, either from love or desperation.

There were various occupations invented during the war, interrupted by "Arms folded", "Arms behind you" and "Hands on heads", while things were given out. 'Ravelling' was a good lesson, which many children were never able to master. A six-inch square of new material was put in front of each child and at the signal these were picked up and ravelling commenced. The idea was to unpick your piece of cloth down to its limit. The threads were then used to stuff pillows for wounded soldiers (perhaps). Clever little me immediately learned that if you started carefully with an outside thread it worked easily. Your ravellings mounted up on your desk and your piece of cloth got smaller and smaller, growing interesting patterns. If you were brilliant you could even vary between squares and oblongs, long sides and short ones. It is true to say that less than 50% ever twigged the principle behind weaving – or even unweaving.

We were taught to write, of course, varying from large chalk figurations in the infants' to more refined pencil, then ink at the age of 9 or 10. Oh! The reminiscences belonging to the acquisition of ink writing, aiming eventually at slanting up, straight down perfection. First the tools – that is to say school nibs, sharp and unresponsive, as likely to leave their trail in the paper as on it. Then there were inkwells, which fitted the holes at the top of the desks from Standard 2 onwards. There was an ink tray per class, which was an unattached shelf of wood with handles each side and the holes ready for the china ink wells.

There were also two staunch and pampered ink monitors, amongst the most favoured citizens of the classroom. They fitted the china cups into the holes in the cloakroom, then walked round and distributed them. They were Machiavellian and could swear that your ink well was perfectly clean, when it was full of disintegrating blotting paper. They could also provide the messy bits drowned in the bottom, so that those dreadful ghosts – blots – and strings of cotton, even string itself, appeared mysteriously across your virgin paper. This meant, "I must not blot, I must not blot" all playtime on my slate, from ten to one hundred times according to my previous history. The nibs were appalling instruments, even when new, and acquired fascinating variations of deadliness when part-used. Not for us the comfort and ease from nibs bought by grown ups.

> "They came as a boon and a blessing to men,
> The Pickwick, the Owl, and the Waverley pen."

This was the ubiquitous advertisement pumped out by the Scottish makers every week. There were also those golden, flexible and right-angled nibs used by the sophisticated.

Then there was blotting paper, scarce and sacrosanct, and definitely never to be written on. Some kids never twigged that, swear as they might, the legitimate use of blotting paper would make the words read backwards instead of forwards. Finally, there was Friday evening collecting and washing out the wells, a proceeding which caused many an ink monitor to let down his hair and lose his job.

Reading – the most essential of all schooling – was taught in various ways, mostly sensibly, but seldom I think for the love of what you read or the knowledge you absorbed. The practice of dividing the words (or letters) into bits, and adding a non-existent 'ur' syllable, to make it easy to pronounce, was absolutely in vogue. So we had c says cur, a says a, t says tur, so we get curator, or do we?

Of course there were never enough books or other reading material. I remember on first being introduced to the 'big school', being given a very thick Linson bound, red Grimm's Fairy Tales and shunted happily into a corner of the room while the class was taught the art of reading. Mention a digraph to these dyed-in-the-wool 'sounding' experts and they ran a mile.

One thing that operated against church schools was the fact that the teachers were paid by the state while everything else, building, furniture, books and any apparatus was provided by the church. So you might well have a good teacher, but no books and a roof that did not keep the rain out. Guess what? What books there were tended to be about missionaries as well as historic figures – so we had burnt cakes, the tide that would not turn, as well as the poor little piccaninnies of darkest Africa who had no clothes to wear. So obviously the humanities were taught by word of mouth with an occasional picture to help. Geography, history and English were thus served and science had not been heard of. Stay! At about Standard 3 the friendly teacher confided in us that in future we must have 'object' lessons (a government decree) and I suppose this close devotion to the properties of anything could be the beginning of scientific enquiry, and oddly enough our first object, which was a brick, prompted a fair amount of enthusiasm, at least in me. I suppose we were glad to enjoy the actual solid existence of the chosen 'object'.

Poetry, strangely enough, was the lifeblood of our English lessons – not always good and often dictated by its regular beat.

> "By the shores of Gitche Gumee,
> By the shining Big-Sea-Water,
> Stood the wigwam of Nokomis,
> Daughter of the Moon...."
> (Hiawatha's Childhood by H.W. Longfellow)

> "It was the schooner Hesperus,
> That sailed the wintry sea;
> And the skipper had taken his little daughter,
> To bear him company."
> (The Wreck of the Hesperus by H.W. Longfellow)

> "The Assyrian came down like the wolf on the fold,
> His cohorts were gleaming in purple and gold;
> And the sheen of their spears was like stars on the sea,
> When the blue wave rolls nightly on deep Galilee."
> (The Destruction of Sennacherib by Lord Byron)

There was also Wordsworth's Daffodils, and my earliest, and I think my favourite, Little brown brother, oh little brown brother, are you awake in the dark? by Edith Nesbitt.

English of course was a cinch because of its closeness to stories, and there was a great deal of correction of the spoken word as well as the written one. There was spelling, an ever-present possibility of teacher-oppression and the accumulation of marks. Many exercises were pleasant because games were being invented and played. But, would you believe it, by Standard 4 when we were ten or eleven years old, our school, at least, had launched into grammar, and I mean just that. We learned to parse words and analyse sentences. I loved standing at my desk and counting on my fingers behind me the eleven things that could be said about some words. For example: The apple is a common noun. It is the subject of the sentence. It fell. Where? In the orchard. How? Squashily. Why? Because it was over-ripe. When? In October. That was adverbs disposed of, then there were adjectives to be similarly dealt with, a triumph if like me you had the power to do it. The analysis was pretty simple – short sentences with the necessary subject, object, and verb. Many of us travelled further and when I reached the High School we had it all to learn again.

Of course the bedrock of all useful learning was arithmetic, known as sums. A multiplicity of tables was sung or shouted, as far as the sixteen times if you were bright. They included remarkable things like the avoirdupois (weights table), lengths up to and including miles, and a mysterious 'square' measure which proved difficult to visualise unless your dad had an allotment. There were various curiosities invented by sharp teachers to fit the occasion; such as the penny-halfpenny table (stamps for letters cost just that) and the half crown table (dead easy). Numbers used were often astronomical, to keep us busy, and it was commonplace to be asked to convert £1,850.10s into pence, or vice versa. Many of these exercises gave one a great feeling of satisfaction when one saw the ordained order of working reach from the top to the bottom of the page. I believe 90% of all sums were offered as figures, and only a few Class 6 girls ever had to translate 'problems' into figures – in fact into reality.

Otherwise there were various hand-centred lessons like the ravellings, drawing with thick coloured school crayons on dark paper, knitting, sewing, creating with strips of paper which could be used more than once, like all stationery in abysmally short supply.

When I proudly announced to my teacher that I could now knit she was quite annoyed because it wasn't my turn. Anyway, she was able to put down the little upstart, who had been carefully watching her next door neighbour and learning to knit, by pointing out to her that she was not in fact knitting but casting on. I had to pull it all out.

These were days of triumph and embarrassment mixed with head inspections by the Nitty Norah. Many notes were handed out for cleaning up at the Centre – that was the ultimate embarrassment. I managed to escape this, by a word in the ear of my mum from the nurse. I was in fact infested moderately, which was the beginning of a schism between me and Dad who would not allow me near him. Much work and pints of liquid made from Quassia chips eventually cleared me ready for the High School, where I spent many an agitated moment either feeling or imagining crawling sensations. That I suppose really marked my big leap forward to unimagined freedom and schoolgirl engagements.

Orthodox religion was in control of the day schools, of which there were five or six attached to churches and only two run by the state. As far as St Mary's was concerned that meant Old Testament on Monday and Wednesday and New Testament on Tuesday and Thursday. Friday was a constant repetition of articles in which we 'believed', the Catechism, the Hail Mary, the Nunc Dimitis and the 23rd Psalm. What a waste of breath was the Catechism, though I can still say it!

The vicar could come in when he liked and give a lesson, but I don't ever remember him doing so. In addition there was a grand exam taking all day (nearly) but sweetened by the school closing at two o'clock. We were always amused because there was a very intelligent Jewish girl, blond, whose parents kept the local chippie. She insisted on being at the New Testament lessons and gave the school much support.

Apart from the Christmas treat, the high point of the church's year was Whit-Thursday which involved a procession from the school to the church, followed by the day off. This meant two or three hundred rowdy extras galloping across the road to the beach.

## Sundays, Religion and Church

My family belonged to the Church of England, dutifully doing the minimum of attendance at church services and Sunday school. The latter was, of course, mainly a way of disposing of the kids on a Sunday morning, in case the boredom of a Sunday should prove too much for them. We were in the parish of Holy Trinity, but did not attend their day school. What happened at Sunday school was always in the balance, as the groups were taken by good-hearted volunteers who tended to change rapidly, according to the behaviour of the children. I myself actually became one, at the earnest request of my mum, and because I knew I would be released from such bondage when I went to college. Usually the whole gathering sang a hymn and said a prayer, then dispersed according to age to torment in various ways the teachers, who knew nothing much, though the less vulnerable ones soon learnt that if they told or read stories they were safe. At one time we had Sunday school record books, with sections that would be filled each week with an adhesive, commemorative stamp. If your book was not reasonably filled you didn't get invited to the Christmas treat. This led to one of my crafty brother's most successful scams. He liked my company on his Sunday morning escapades, and somehow got hold of a complete year's supply of stamps. Regularly, therefore, I could show my parents the stamp for the day stuck in the right place. Thus was formed what I suppose was a kind of soothing effect. My parents thought I was safely in Sunday school while I was enjoying myself climbing on the West Hill, and so was Lionel, with the added pleasure of having again pulled off a successful diddling of authority.

Only one thing spoilt it for me. That was my ever-present pricking of conscience.

The Christmas treat was always looked forward to, because people did not ever have parties themselves, so this was the annual letting down of hair and stuffing of young stomachs. Some sort of entertainment was on offer – Father Christmas, a conjuror, or clown – but the grub was the thing and we all went home with the traditional bun and orange.

Sunday morning at home was always the same. Grandma came across and organised a huge bake-up. As we grew older my sister was allowed to assist and, after Grandma's death, took over completely. Apart from the Sunday joint sizzling in the oven, and a good spread of a limited type of vegetable, an apple pie was always de rigueur. Rock buns had to be made every week, small fairy cakes, a big fruitcake, and a popular and late introduction by my sister, of coconut pyramids, both white and pink. The whole house was warm and friendly and happiness reigned. There was never any discord between Mum and Grandma, never any suggestion that my mother was being devalued in any way. She was happy with the mainline cooking for the rest of the week. The other chore she was saved was darning the socks and stockings. Yes, we even darned stockings in those days – they tended to be made of wool, cotton or lisle. Grandma was so efficient it eventually rubbed off on to me and I really enjoyed doing a perfect darn – just as well as it was in the time of black gym stockings and much falling over, resulting in grazed knees.

We were, in fact, limited in what we might do on a Sunday. Reading stories was looked on doubtfully unless they were missionary tales. Needlework was absolutely not allowed. Playing card games was forbidden. So what was left? In the winter when the fire had been lit in the best bedroom it was not so bad, as a general feeling of well being reigned and there was a chance to chat. Of course, gradually over the years the forbidden activities crept in, and the very last was sewing.

In the summer there was the chance of visiting relations or taking walks, short or long. Father was dragged to church on the four most important days of the church's year; apart from that he opted out in favour of sleep. Mum often went to Evensong and took me with her. I could not say whether the sermons preached were good or abysmal, as I could not listen to them. Being stuck in the most uncomfortable pews something else had got to be done. I found a lot of interest in the first half of the Book of Common Prayer. Many times I followed the instructions on how to find out when Easter would fall in any given year. Unfortunately it came on a different date every year. However, it used up quite an appreciable amount of time. Then there was a list of people one must not marry which gave much food for thought. What is wrong with your wife's sister's niece for example? Suffice to say, time passed in a more or less edifying way. (Incidentally, the small boards attached to the ends of some pews bearing the warning 'Sidesman', or 'Verger', or something similar were painted by my father over fifty years ago.)

My brother was persuaded to join the choir, which in those days was paid a small sum. Every Friday night (practice night) Lionel proudly presented Mum with a quarter pound of tea out of his earnings. One fateful day the choirmaster came into the shop to say how sorry he was that my brother had left the choir. The dreadful thing was that he had still made his gift to Mum on a Friday night. Where did the money come from? A question that arose several more times during his young life, causing great sorrow to me and great worry to our parents.

In our parish we had district visitors who no doubt helped families in trouble, but to us were the benefactors who presented us with an Annual at Christmas, a Chatterbox for Lionel, a Sunday for me. The Chatterbox usually finished up in my possession. It was an education in itself. It printed poetry, not merely verse, often a full page set in a really beautiful decorated border. I learnt a good deal through reading and re-reading them. There were short extracts from Shakespeare, usually a set of songs culled from the plays. Even Milton was printed and I could repeat L'Allegro by the time I was nine but drew the line at Il Penseroso, which was surely what the poet intended. There was also a serial story which I liked and all kinds of puzzles, especially the rebus which I enjoyed and also invented for myself. It was a brilliant magazine and ran as an Annual for many years. By the sixties it was very sought after in the secondhand book trade. Sunday was a pale reflection of Chatterbox, and the book they finally gave the household was Little Folks, a literary journey downhill.

## Entertainments

As it was a seaside place Hastings always had to provide entertainment – formal or otherwise. In its heyday when the carriage trade was the cause of prosperity in the town there were two much sought after spots where you could see and be seen, both highly respectable libraries. Later when St Mary-in-the-Castle had been built there was a promenade beneath it that could be used in bad weather.

For the ordinary people there was the frequent arrival of a circus or a menagerie. The small area next to the Town Hall often housed them. One wonders how such a small spot could contain so much. Real roundabouts with galloping horses on a spiral pole were as expected, swing-boats to terrify the squeamish, coconut shies and all the expected fun of the fair were crowded into this small space. I remember watching, with absolute belief and fascination, Buffalo Bill riding madly round and round shooting up Red Indians. I just refused to belief that Buffalo Bill was dead, and anyhow he had lived in America.

By the end of the 1890's two piers had been built, one in Hastings, one in St Leonards. In the first, minstrel troupes appeared with blackened faces, straw hats and white gloves – they did a kind of 'knees up', leaning over backwards at a frightening angle, and sang:

> "Come on and hear, come on and hear
> Alexander's Ragtime Band.
> Come on and hear, come on and hear,
> It's the best band in the land.
> If you want to hear dat Swanee Ribber played in Ragtime
> Come on and hear, come on and hear
> Alexander's Ragtime Band."

It seemed more popular than Pierrot troupes, which were beginning to feel old fashioned as the new rhythms came in.

St Leonards pier had a roller skating rink on which I tried unsuccessfully to skate – egged on by Lionel. Both piers had a ballroom and a theatre for visiting performers. It was at one of these that my parents were watching a drama about the White Slave Traffic. The heroine, having been abducted by the villain, was stood on a plinth for auction. The hero was in the audience with (we were assured) £500. Alas the bidding went to £600 and my mum, almost bursting with excitement and dread, stood up in the stalls and shrieked "£650!" which rather broke the tension and brought the house down.

Minor trade fairs were held on both piers, and I attended, transfixed, an early account of the expedition to the South Pole with rather primitive pictures. It was, of course, very close in time.

Moving pictures were a sensation, and were first shown upstairs above an empty shop in York Buildings. I was taken, but removed howling. The hero and heroine communicated by letters, which were left in a hole in a bank.

Unfortunately a snake had chosen to lay its eggs there, which were hatching and the heroine was about to put her hand literally in a 'nest of vipers'. I couldn't stand it. I later became an addicted cinema goer with my brother. There were at one time at least seven cinemas flourishing in the town, one, a flea-pit, at the bottom of our street. We visited them all, and knew how to get into the Public Hall Cinema without paying, by bashing up the bar of the fire exit, going in and hovering round the toilets till we thought it safe to walk in and take our seats. Our usual haunt, though, was the Cinema de Luxe on the sea front. This rather grand red-brick affair, had been built as a Music Hall, but Music Hall had died. For fourpence we got a seat on a wooden bench with no back and the pleasure of a piano accompaniment by an old lady who also acted as something of a disciplinarian when our stamping became too loud.

Some of the shows that appealed to young children were, of course, cartoon films, and these were not very glamorous. The first well defined character I can remember was Felix.

> "Felix kept on walking,
> Kept on walking still.
> With his hands behind him
> You will always find him."

And indeed you did, walking away from his latest calamity. I think he was the first progenitor of Mickey, but then he was a lonely black cat on a plain white background.

The first humans I remember were two pairs of somewhat lugubrious figures drawn in black – Mutt & Jeff and Weary Willie & Tired Tim, who always seemed to be waiting for Godot even in those days. Each pair started off early comics: Chips, drawn on pink paper and Comic Cuts, drawn on pale green. Soon new characters and new situations developed till the young generation was spoilt for choice. Later, Tiger Tim's Weekly produced a famous school for animals which went on for years and spawned some of the earliest annuals. By now, of course, a kind of to and fro connection between the cinema and the press had developed, and daily adventures of Pip, Squeak, and Wilfred, Oojah the Elephant and many others littered the kitchen floor. The Keystone Cops rushed madly through most households, and stalled every time on a level crossing. Individual comedians became popular, especially a particularly wall-eyed one (Ben Turpin) who worried me to death, and then – Charlie.

Children adored his early grotesque and rather surrealist shorts, their violence, terror, and eventually the restoration of calm – right always conquered. The Chaplin logos – stick, bowler, moustache and big boots – were a stroke of brilliance on someone's part, and were destined to remain with him as a sentimental reference point even to his last films. Charlie did indeed become a children's hero – entering their street games and their songs – sometimes unprintable. We skipped to:

"Charlie Chaplin went to France
To teach the ladies how to dance."

We bounced balls to other ditties:

"Oh the sun shines bright on Charlie Chaplin,
His boots are cracking, for the want of blacking,
And his little baggy trousers, they want mending,
Before they send him
To the Dardanelles."

And a true childish sympathy was felt for all his trials and escapades. We forgot quite soon the huge black-eyed bruiser who was his enemy, and the rather insipid little girl he fell in love with.

We followed the exploits of William S. Hart, our chosen cowboy and ostracised Tom Mix, whom we regarded as a bit of a sissy. We also followed, spellbound, the serial stories, with Pearl White or someone similar, either tied to the rails while an express thundered towards her (till next week) or hanging from a rope over a chasm, while the rope gradually frayed. Our favourite was not, however, a tale of beauty in danger, but one called The Mystery Man, which I think must have been produced with early special effects.

When the fashion for Minstrel Shows faded a more or less permanent Concert Party took over, and played for several seasons running. They were known as Wallis Arthur's and played in a marquee on the ground next to the Town Hall every evening, and in the park bandstand on week-end afternoons. We found the marquee easy to access by loosening a guy-rope to crawl in, and then climbing quietly up inside the scaffolding of the tiered seats at the back, and taking our places on the top row, which was seldom full. We enjoyed the first half of the programme and then lined up with the rest of the audience to collect a Pass Out Ticket in the interval. Although we then felt ourselves to be legitimate we did not enjoy the second half as much as the first because the players discarded their Pierrot costumes for evening dress – this made everything more refined. We did not always relish Come you back to Mandalay and The green eye of the little yellow god forever gazes down, and still less There's a brown bird singing down the la-ane, and other female invitations to romance. We went for the hurly-burly of comic songs and sketches, often directed surprisingly mildly against Italians (plenty of macaroni and ice creams), Germans (obviously sausages) and Spaniards ("I'll raise a bunion on his Spanish onion if I catch him bending tonight"). I cannot remember any patriotic songs, although they were of course being sung everywhere as we were in the middle of a war.

Wallis Arthur faded – and as a very handsome White Rock Pavilion was built during the slump, a new kind of superior concert party appeared – the Fol de Rols. As a teenager, now leaving my childish tastes for entertainment behind, I became an avid supporter. But everything was too organised and substantial for any back door entrance – we had to pay.

My really favourite offering was the funny man's pirate song – in costume with moustache:

> "Then I snap my finger – ha, ha, ha, ha !
> And I snap the other one – ho, ho, ho, ho!
> I don't care should the parent pine,
> Once aboard the lugger and the girl is mine.
> Then I set my sails and sail away,
> No pirate e'er was cooler,
> For wher-e'er I go, I fear no foe,
> On the good ship Yac-ki Hic-ki Doo La."
> (Laugh)

(The audience always supplied a choric note after a short pause.)

If visitors or residents ever had any spare pennies there were always the slot machines. These were not to keep you gainfully employed as now, but to amuse you. The first I remember was in fact live. An old Italian lady with a head-scarf sporting coins round the edge, had a cage on wheels just by the Queens Hotel. This contained canaries (or could they have been budgerigars?) and on the reception of a penny, these would pick a folded paper out of a little box and offer it through the bars. This contained a prediction of your future life. The mechanical slot machines I remember included a house on fire with flames seen through the windows and firemen

Reproduced by kind permission of Francis Day And Hunter Ltd., who own the copyright of this sheet music.

# It Was Like This

Reproduced by kind permission of Francis Day And Hunter Ltd.,
who own the copyright of this sheet music.

running up and down ladders. A favourite was a beheading by guillotine with plenty of blood. There were always a few racier ones which children were shooed away from. Again, the trick was to position yourself just behind a prosperous child and wait for his guardian to put a coin in.

There were other machines which did not put on a show, but foretold your future. One of these had a handprint on which you stretched your hand, and on the reception of a penny lots of little pins (blunt) rose and returned, and thus read your hand. This was rather creepy and I almost believed it. I will finish with the famous sailor who looked solemnly at you, and warningly intoned "Sydney Knows" before shrieking with laughter.

## Shops and Shopping

There were quite a lot of small grocers in the town – ours was the World's Stores. I spent many hours shopping there and quite enjoyed it. It was near home in Queens Road, and smelt very nice. There were half-cylinders of enamelled metal with lids that crashed down. They were well decorated and held raisins, currants, dates and all kinds of dry goods, like rice and sugar. The shops did not buy bags to sell these, but kept large sheets of tough but soft paper which could be easily formed into 'pokes' or triangular pockets. Hence, of course, 'sugar paper', used in primary schools for painting. There was a coffee roaster and grinder to add to the pleasant smells. Cheese was offered in enormous hunks which were cut up with a cheese wire, but the grocer also had by him a small metal tool, like an apple corer, with which he removed a plug of cheese for you to taste. I cannot remember a bacon slicer, so maybe this was still done by hand. Butter was in a huge pile on a marble slab, from which the grocer removed the approximate weight with two flat pats, rather like ping-pong bats but square. He weighed it on greased paper and added or subtracted small lumps as required. Then it was patted into bricks, sometimes marked with stripes or flowers from the embossing on the butter pats.

There were a number of these branches of all-purpose shops, some – like the Maypole Dairy – specialising in dairy foods. I can well remember an incident during the first world war when I was sent to collect Grandma's butter (we gave her all our butter coupons), and finding a crowded mob in the Maypole all waving coupons and shouting. I think they were afraid the butter was going to run out. I, six years old, was at the back crying and submerged, when a strong man by me lifted me bodily and passed me over people's heads to the front to be served. I was overwhelmed and still think it to have been one of the nicest things that ever happened to me. There was, as well, the Home and Colonial Stores and sundry one-off shops, not members of a chain. These tended to be rather superior, like Amoores, and a bit expensive.

Milk, bread and fish came to your doorstep. Coal was a different matter; many people didn't have it delivered in bulk, having nowhere to put it, and not enough ready cash to pay for it. So, Lionel, like many another young boy, took the pushchair up to the coal yard by the station, and brought back maybe half or one hundredweight at a time. Another deviation from a respectable norm was to send a child down to the baker's, Bonenblust's, with a pillowcase to buy stale bread. Mum would not sink so low, but we were sent down for 'threepenn'orth of stale chokers', meaning buns. Because my brother was a mate of her sons, Mrs Bonenblust often slipped a Swedish pastry or other delight into my bag.

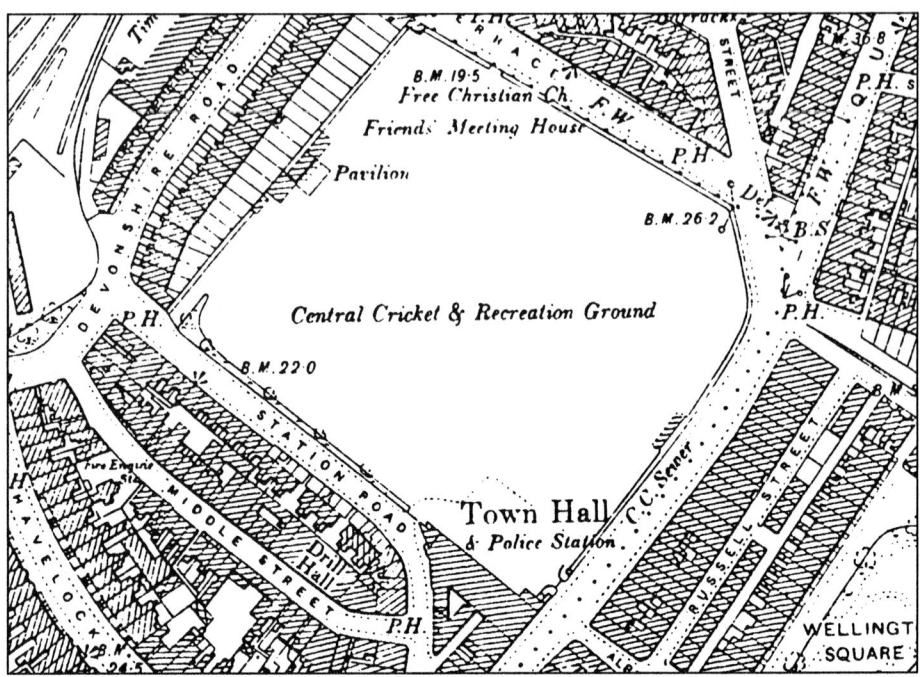

*Illustration 15 - Map showing proximity of Middle Street to the Cricket Ground. Reproduced from O.S.map of 1987*

*Illustration 16 - The Cricket Ground
(Station Road and Middle Street to left of picture)
Reproduced by kind permission of Hastings Museum.*

# Surrounding Areas

As soon as a child reached the ripe old age of about five, at first cautiously, he began wandering near and far to range his stamping ground. Hastings was, and is, ideal for this; there are so many public spaces, natural or man-made.

## The Cricket Ground

Nearest to us was the Cricket Ground, a mere step away, behind the back of the street, with only the single-sided development of Station Road to separate us. On the other side of this was a waist-high wall topped by railings, which ran round three sides of a large, beautifully kept green space. This was the Cricket Ground, made upon part of the low-lying estuary of the Priory Streams. The grass was always lush, but it was liable to flooding when high tides and storms coincided.

Besides the actual cricket table there was a wide expanse of well-kept land, so that the grounds could be used for other outdoor pursuits such as school and town sports days. There were two major gates, a pavilion, an infrequently used tearoom and the usual lavatories.

The Trust who had instituted the grounds had made a clause that every Monday evening until 9 o'clock, the place should be open freely for all the children of the district to play. Most of the streets were fairly poverty stricken and there were plenty of kids to take advantage of this charitable clause and play all kinds of games there, even trying to emulate W. G. Grace, Duleepsinhji and Ranjitsinhji who had played there for the County.

A boy of whom we were all proud, Alan Oakman, was apprenticed to the groundsman as soon as he left school at 14, soon played cricket like a pro, and eventually became a demon bowler, both for Sussex and for England; an example of when a child from a very ordinary family, living in a back alley, rises above his circumstances if given the opportunity.

The eastern side was filled with the back three or four stories of a row of boarding houses, with wonderful views of County matches. The houses were quite elegant, and by some quirk of fate the whole row is still standing complete.

Round about the twenties it was decided to put a row of tennis courts on the side abutting Queens Road and soon a row of shops. It is true that the occasional flooding soon made the Kent v. Sussex County matches a bit unreliable, so that they later moved to Brighton, followed by all the County Fixtures.

(Fairly recently the powers that be, the Town Clerk and the Council, decided that such a beautiful centre for the town was useless – there was no money in it – and they proposed a shopping mall. There was much opposition, and some support, and the altercation went on for many years, involving some very dodgy incidents – for instance at one point the Town Clerk and Accountant were expected to sail out beyond the three mile limit to meet the developers to sign the contract. To cut a long and bitter story short, concrete swallowed up the grass and the shopping mall was built. The Town Clerk retired immediately. This decision also meant that a telephone exchange now stands on the spot where I was born and the street has almost entirely disappeared, except for the pubs top and bottom.)

## The West Hill

The West Hill was, and is, a suitable area for all ages. The high escarpment of sandstone rocks, very climbable in some parts, difficult and dangerous in others, catered for large and small. One found a route over the rocks, which became one's own property, and sometimes this led to an altercation between two parties claiming the same way. This rock was very friable, good for carving one's name with a bit of broken glass. However, it only took about six months for it to be worn completely smooth.

On the top of West Hill was the Ladies' Parlour. This was a flattened area of grass surrounded by banks. It has been suggested that it was the old jousting ground of the Castle (which stands beside it across a deep ravine). My mother warned us not to go up after dusk, because the surrounding banks made comfortable support for couples intent on more than breathing the invigorating night air. The rocks were the centre-piece of a large area of grass, a bit wild in early days, but kept beautifully cut and rolled by the Council now.

A big attraction to us small fry was St Clement's Caves. In our day there was no lighting. The custodian was a burly man in navy blue serge covered with candle grease droppings. It cost fourpence to be shown round, but he would sometimes let us in for twopence, or nothing at all if he'd been out for his lunchtime drink. He carried an object like a ping-pong bat on which two candles were stuck. Sometimes one or both burned out, but he kept a supply in his pocket. There was a fairly big central cave out of which led sundry passages, big and small. The whole thing was a bit scary.

(At a later date, someone held a dance there and that led to a regular Saturday hop, with a resident group, The Jazz Caverners, who are still blowing their trumpets today. Alas! Alas! Alas! Eventually the town realised they had here a nice little earner, electricity was laid on, boutiques were opened, wax figures of smugglers were planted at strategic intervals and an excruciating sound system was installed.

During the second world war the caves had a useful function. A number of people started to take shelter there from the raids. Instead of blocking them off, the authorities had the sense to open them up, install facilities such as lavatories, a cook-house, and even an altar. So for many people life went on as before, but underground. Some merely slept there, but many went in and did not come out again till the end of the war – my old Aunt Bessie being one of them. A little girl was actually born there, and christened, inevitably, Cavina.)

## East Hill

Looking from the West Hill across the valley that contains the Old Town one sees the East Hill, bigger and more distant, but on the whole less interesting for children. Both hills were fitted with lifts in the nineteenth century, but now we must call them Cliff Railways, more elevated, I suppose. Pun intended. We never had the money to use them, but there were many ways of getting to the top by various hills and steps.

The East Hill was reached from the Old Town by a hundred or so stone steps, by the lift, and by sundry ways from more inland. There was nothing on it but wind and grass and one bank-enclosed space called Frenchman's Land, the haunted patch popularly supposed to have been enclosed to keep prisoners in the Napoleonic Wars. At any rate during the first world war it became allotments, and reverted to wild grass and shrubs. (Recently, it has been taken in hand, the grass mowed, the fractured hedges encouraged to grow again, and the whole area turned into a picnic ground with tables and benches and a couple of hearths for barbecues. A really good job was made of this and it is not unusual for a garden rose to appear on the bushes, or an old tool to make its way up from beneath the grass.)

If you wished to push on eastwards a stretch of country continued for eight or nine miles, and included the famous glens.

## Ecclesbourne and Fairlight Glens

Of course the places I mention now were not part of the explorations of the young alone, but also of accompanying grown ups. They all provide reminiscences of a rich childhood.

The East Hill led on to Ecclesbourne Glen and Fairlight Glen. The first at least was within easy reach when accompanied by my brother. Here a steep, muddy, sandy path led into a wooded ravine. Amongst the bushes lived the Hermit. We were always dubious about him, though not frightened. He seemed harmless although, viewed on the curve of the hill, against the vast sky, with his gun on his shoulder, he looked most impressive. His home was a sort of half cave in the rock with an extension on the front built of packing cases, and in front of that a patch where he grew potatoes. The whole thing was invisible unless you knew where to look. His regime was usually to visit the Old Town dustbins at dawn (not that he would find much there), then shoot or snare a rabbit and stew it up on a wood fire. No-one knew anything about him, but he was visited by the blind maker, Fred Rolfe, who indeed found his dead body, or what the rats had left of it.

The stream that ran through the glen came to a dead drop of about 20 feet, and made a tinkling waterfall. Iron staples were let into the rock face so that the bold could climb down to the beach. It was possible to walk on the rocks below the cliff as far as the town – but many people were cut off by the tide and panicked. A steep climb up the other side led to further hills and small glens via the Lovers' Seat – a place of romance even to us kids. This was a space in the cliff face with a wooden seat thoughtfully installed, and above it a huge flat tongue of rock (which was eventually blown down and smashed up in a gale). The lover in question was a Warren from Warren Glen, who met her young man in secret when he put ashore in a small boat from his cutter. They both died unromantically ashore, of old age.

Fairlight was like the previous glen, but deeper and bigger in every way. After a struggle through the undergrowth and mud you came out into the open at the top of a hog's back, down which you came to the sea, that is if you were a boy and bold. This little sister used to scramble down the side, coming out pretty filthy at the bottom. The contours of this part of the cliff were much changed after the second world war.

From the sea, the cliffs and the whole area were mined in case of invasion. It says much for the efficiency of the British Army that there was reputedly only one map of the layout, which was blown up with the Commanding Officer as he was cutting a path through the barbed wire. So for many years the cows and ramblers who wandered all over the place were blown up sporadically. At last the War Office decided enough was enough and sent the Engineers in to clear the place. So for a whole summer there were loud explosions and at the end of it our precious hog's back was gone. The clay puddles remained, yellow, white, grey and black, but nobody now needed to pipe-clay their front step.

Climbing out of Fairlight Glen there were several miles of high land, known as the Firehills, some say because beacons were lit there in times of war, some say it was the flaming yellow of the gorse that gave them that name. There were various small installations and lookout posts belonging to the Coast Guards and eventually at Cliff End the path dropped down to Pett Level and the beginning of the Romney Marsh (famous for smugglers) which extended as far as Hythe.

Pett Level was the favourite resort of the Knights family when we were young – all, including the baby in the pushchair and Grandma wearing a black sateen apron to gather winkles, walked the ten miles or so, up hill and down dale, often carrying a frying pan and bacon and sausages. We gathered plenty of wood amongst the jetsam on the beach. It was always bleached and burned with a blue flame, spurting red sparks. There were many strong wooden breakwaters, which had been there for many years and which were ideal for climbing. There was dark coloured sand, almost red, which made the place rather exotic. There were deep and shallow pools, sharp and rounded rocks and areas of soft clay which was delightful to squidge between the toes, but terrifying if it turned out to be deep. We were haunted by our reading, like The Hound of the Baskervilles where foolish (or wicked) characters were sucked down, a situation which really held horrors for me, especially when the morass had reached the victim's nose. There were, fairly far out, wooden posts and staves, which we believed were the remains of a prehistoric forest. In fact they were the timbers of the warship Anne which was defeated in battle at Beachy Head and then rounded the coast as far as Pett Level. The Master sent his men ashore, afterwards setting the ship on fire and destroying everything above decks.

This marked our eastward journeying, but on the way we might have stayed and explored Camber Castle, which was bare and boring. At other times we spent the day at Pevensey Castle, very popular because of the large spaccs within the perimeter walls, or at Bodiam Castle, the perfect example of what a castle should look like with its moat and drawbridge, or less frequently Herstmonceux which we hardly counted as a castle because it was made of red brick. We also made long walks on a Sunday, usually finishing up gratifyingly at a pub, where we were happy to sit outside with a packet of biscuits and, on lucky days, a lemonade. I always opted if possible for an enormous arrowroot biscuit, so big they cost twopence for one. We dragged home tired out, clutching, at the right season, a bunch of bluebells, fragile wood anemones or primroses, and then our booty had to be sorted and watered and arranged, a job that usually fell to me.

## The Sea

Of course a very great influence on all our lives was the existence of the sea with its bonus of space and air. As children we had an opportunity to run and to explore which is denied to town-bound children now. There was also a rather vague feeling of living on the edge of things, though what influence that had on us I cannot say. But there it was, the sea: every day, everlasting, ever changing; and the amount of 'science' we absorbed would have satisfied and surprised a modem setter of standards. The sea itself with its many changing colours taught us to anticipate its movements like a sailor, though we were often drenched through running under a high wave, but at least we learned not to get washed away.

Middle Street was literally five minutes' walk from the sea. All night long one could hear the pounding of the waves. There was always too, the rattle of the pebbles in the undertow and the wind, howling or whispering all the time. Something was always on the move.

You could judge by its appearance which sand was perfect for digging, or for building castles – either to smash or to stand on for as long as possible as the tide surrounded them. You could tell which sand was good to draw on, and which to squidge between your toes where slurry had formed in pools lined with clay. You learned which rocks to run on, which to tread carefully on so as not to slip, and where to learn to ride your bike without danger.

All this and more could be experienced from the actual appearance of the environment. And then you came to the life of the coast, both moving and inanimate. Seaweed could be collected, floated to show off its beautiful shapes, dried and pressed. Efforts at fishing could be made from rod and line to shrimping nets and prawn gins. Individual aquariums could be made in rock pools with shrimps, starfish, winkles, green crabs and many other creatures. Some could stay in your chosen pool, like limpets and sea anemones with their squashy bodies and coloured tentacles.

Little attention was paid to boats, except for noting on the horizon the distant smudge of a tanker or a liner. There was no shipping close in, till you came to the rather fragile rowboats parked on the beach to be hired by visitors. There were, however, two large wind-powered boats, known as the yachts, which plied for visitors to take a ride. "Who's for a trip in the Albertine?" Could the other one have been called The Skylark?

*Illustration 17 - Muriel with cousin Molly on a beach outing*

The boatmen were a fairly grumpy lot as their little boats were constantly climbed on and over. The real sea-dogs were the fishermen, whose boats were well protected. They were, in those days, almost a race apart – so clannish that when one of their daughters married a non-fisherman she was described ruefully as having 'gone over the side'. The faces of the fishermen were brown and rather alike; they were often blond with blue eyes, and sported a single earring to prevent drowning. Some of their speech varied from normal Sussex. They could not, until recently, pronounce 'th' but replaced it with 'd'. They referred to everyone as 'young un'. Even their grandfathers were called 'my old young un'. This was a strange local habit. Even when referring to his aged father an old-timer would address him as 'little old young'un'. I decided later that it was somehow connected with Dutch. Reading a number of Dutch thrillers I found the lads called each other 'Jongen', equivalent to 'mate'.

They, or their wives, tended to present themselves as hard done by. "The poor dear 'earts", as their wives called them, "haven't had a single night's fishing this week." There was always a note of disbelief in the office when

*Illustration 18 - The net shops. Etching by Kathleen Crozier (circa 1942)*

they went to sign on. If the weather was so bad that they couldn't go out it was counted as a day's unemployment, and you can imagine the arguments about whether they should be allowed to pick up their dole money on a day when the weather could not make its mind up. They spent a lot of time on the beach leaning, or repairing their nets or sorting the catch. There was a powerful sense of togetherness, not least when storms were brewing and they risked their lives in truly hazardous conditions.

The lifeboat in those days was kept in a shed on land, and it had to be man-handled to the most suitable spot for launching. So there was often entertainment and occupation in pulling the boat up, or down, over its greasy launching boards. If it was only a practice alarm, a single maroon was fired and young and old came running. If two maroons went off that meant it was the real thing. Toughies, including my brother, might cadge a night on a lugger, but were usually sorry after.

The Winkle Club – a charitable organisation founded by a group of fishermen – had a number of things happening, including a lavish Christmas party. Various honoured invitees, including the Lord Warden and the Queen, on demand of "Winkle up," were called upon to produce their winkle (a facsimile of the sea creature), or pay a fine. The Queen's was said to be gold.

Another attraction was an elderly man with one arm and a bent fork – an ex fisherman? He drew wonderful scenes in the sand – of public buildings – about three times longer than himself, that were filled with textures and details. People threw down pennies from the promenade. It was a brilliant and much appreciated performance. I have seen children in tears as the sea slowly came in and wiped out the Houses of Parliament, which he rapidly renewed the next day.

There was also a Punch and Judy show on the beach. The promenade at this point did a sort of hiccup which left a pocket of space for entertainment, so morning and afternoons the Punch and Judy man put up his booth and the kids assembled, sitting on the stones or standing round the edge. The Punch and Judy lady went round with a collecting box very grumpily indeed, except to those children whose parents she noticed and she recognised in the audience.

The other grown-ups were treated with respect. Any child who made a noise, or who made the wrong repartee, was ordered – with no authority – off that part of the beach. The repartee expected in those days was pale and thin compared with the volume encouraged today. Simple remarks were treasured and laughed at with real enthusiasm, like the mispronunciation of the word 'cememitry' and the accusation, "He threw the baby out of the window. Wot a pity, wot a pity, wot a pity." It was all enhanced by the small metal ring held in the puppeteer's mouth.

Dog Toby was everyone's favourite. He seemed the epitome of good nature and good behaviour compared with the other scallywags, and his ruffle was always clean and starched. Other props seemed to be used here (as well as in whatever language or country the performance was to be found), a baby, Judy, an alligator, a string of sausages, a frying pan, a policeman, a ghost, a coffin and a gravedigger were usually present. In the words of a famous Sunday newspaper, "The whole of human life was there."

Old man Hubbard was a well known character who, dressed in a seedy morning coat and a top hat, stood in all weathers on the Punch and Judy beach, when it was not occupied by the Punch and Judy man. He preached hell fire and damnation to all sinners. His son, Bobby Hubbard, appeared not to fear the horrors to come himself. Perhaps because he once told us that Old Hubbard was not his real father.

There were many other spasmodic events happening on the beach, Biddy Stonham, the man in the tub, the occasional minstrel, the Sally Army holding noisy services and selling the War Cry in nearby pubs, and other missions for shorter or longer periods.

The arrival from its winter quarters in Bristol of the old paddle steamer was an exciting event and a major attraction for the adults. A day in France – mainly spent in a casino – was quite a usual, though slow, trip.

Thus a very full life was enjoyed by the kids on their home beach. Wandering westward over the Pevensey Marsh and the Crumbles, or eastward over the four hills or through the glens to Cliff End at Pett Level simply extended it.

## The Catholic Grounds

Near home, and westward, was open land belonging to the Convent on the St Leonards side. There had been a bit of town planning before our time, when a huge rock (the White Rock) was blown up to make way for a road parallel with the coast. Above this was cliff again and an area used for many things, including farm land. I think it was Hickman's Fields. As a very small child I was taken to see a hot-air balloon sent up from the top (by a Frenchman, of course).

(Much later all this land was developed as White Rock Gardens with flower beds, tennis courts and, famously, bowling greens. The old farmland was smartened up and became The Oval on which shows, conventions of this and that and the other, and circuses were held. Going inwards across Cambridge Road the fields became farmland again, much of which had previously been a rather posh prep school, Summerfields, with extensive grounds that descended eventually, and rather precipitously, to the railway track. This land has now been divided between a museum, a swimming bath, a police station, a fire station, a hotel and an ambulance headquarters, all useful and, because of the size of the land, not unsightly.)

All this was a free playground when I was young and in the first world war was extensively trenched as a training ground, with firing ranges, and dummy bodies hanging on tripods for bayonet practice. Owing to the length of the perimeter it would have been impossible to fence it in and keep us out. You can imagine the games that could be initiated in such an environment. One of the joys was to search for spent or unused ammunition. At this time there were trams running on ground-level rails. The thing to do was to place a bullet carefully on one of these rails, then wait for a tram to come down from Bohemia. There would follow, sometimes, a loud crack and flash. It was obviously dangerous, but as usual no-one seemed to get hurt. Another thing to do was to place a halfpenny on the tram track when the oncoming tram would flatten it out and spread it to the size of a penny. I never found a shopkeeper gullible enough to accept it.

## Alexandra Park to Old Roar

This was the place in which much of our young lives was spent. It occupied all the land from the estuary of one arm of the Priory Stream right up between two sections of higher ground till it petered out into the country. It was laid out, as the name suggests, in honour of Queen Alexandra and made use of the stream to make a series of connected ponds and reservoirs. The climate here was well protected from wind, and so the gardeners took the opportunity to plant many kinds of non-indigenous trees, which we were glad to climb without realising their botanical values.

In the first park were a boating lake and a large lawn. One side was banked up carefully so you could sit at ease and watch whatever was going on. In our case it was often firework displays with the reflection of the lights in the pond. (Nowadays the firework displays are held where they can be seen by a greater part of the town, such as on the West Hill or the beach.)

*Illustration 19 – The boating lake*

*Illustration 20 – Lake with ducks and black swans*

There were two smaller, more decorative, lakes in this first park, with ducks and black Australian swans. I must have been in my late teens before I realised that the right colour for a swan is white. So, what with the ducks and ducklings to feed, lawns to kick about on, trees to climb, and a pond big enough to learn to paddle your own canoe, there was something for all ages, not only the older people who promenaded the footpaths. No! They did not walk their dogs because dogs were not allowed in and the park was completely surrounded by iron railings. (They were there until some lunatic in the second world war put out a plea for all iron to be surrendered to the Government, and gates and fences were pulled down everywhere. I understand no cannon was ever made from the iron, any more than any planes were made from the aluminium that was given up. It must have been a nice little earner for somebody. The irony of it was that many, including myself, gave up all their cookware and promptly went round to Woolworths to buy new stuff.)

The first pond was a joy, because not only could you go rowing on it if you had the money, but you could sail your yacht on it. If it became stranded in the middle for lack of wind power, you could sometimes get a useful boatman to wade out in his thigh-boots and set it off again. Otherwise a judicial throwing of stones just on the far side of it would get a circular current going to edge it towards land. Unfortunately this operation always attracted every boy in the park, and many did not understand the physics of the procedure, often maliciously aiming at the boat itself. We had a number of small boats, mostly homemade and not very efficient, but our pride was a very large yacht indeed, which had been left behind in a house Dad was decorating. We also had a large box-kite from the same source with which we swanked somewhat on the West Hill, where it suffered many misfortunes with an unreliable wind.

One of my most poignant memories of the park pond must date back to my scarlet fever gap year. In a little dwelling opening on to the Stone Arch lived, from time to time, a small uncommunicative old lady. She was feared or respected because she wore a long black cloak, such a one that was never seen at that time except in a pantomime. Her name, apparently, was Mrs Horne, and occasionally a very small boy stayed with her and then disappeared again. He was, I suppose, about four. I was rising five and bored, with all the other kids at school. So I decided to go to the park, and little velvet-suited Horne decided to follow as there was nobody else available. As soon as we reached the big pond, little Horne decided to fall in. All Hell broke loose, people appeared from everywhere to surround the catastrophe and pull the dripping child out of the pond. Then questions came. Was I supposed to be looking after him? Was I his sister? No, No, No to everything. A small posse took him home the long way down Queens Road, while I ran smartly home the short way over Braybrook Terrace. Next morning a small mob came into the front shop to tell my mother how I had abducted the little boy and then pushed him in the pond. Fortunately Mum kept calm and soothed them down, and I was never punished as they had demanded.

Some of the most enjoyable times of my young life – six years – were two or three years in which somebody – the Council? – organised fetes, using every bit of the park. It was all very cultured and respectable – no jazz, no popular songs, but a dancing display (put on I suppose by one of the many dance schools). There was a great deal of flapping of gauze scarves and falling leaves, all done on a small slanted section which made a stage, and surrounded by bushes which provided changing rooms. On this same stage I saw various sections of the more pastoral Shakespeare plays. On the big lawns a chequer board was marked out and a game of living chess was played on it. The costumes were fun, but if you did not understand the rules of the game the whole thing became incredibly boring.

We knew the three sections of Alexandra Park as the First, Second and Third Parks, though they were all one, with round roads between. They increased in wildness the further they went from the town. In the second part was a so-called Chalybeate Spring, complete with board saying what it contained and what it was good for. The water gushed dark brown out of the wooded bank, assisted by a length of piping, and there was an iron cup on a chain for your use. My nursing aunt believed in its claims and always took a bottle full home with her to London. It was a fun place to visit, not less because the little enclosed side path was nearly always waterlogged. We reckoned that whatever good it might do you, it would be increased by the number of times it passed through the pipe, so our method was to fill the iron cup and throw the water back up the pipe to pick up more of its healing properties. You can imagine how wet we all became as the water was thrown in the wrong direction.

This part of the Park had, and has, some beautiful trees and bushes and dozens of squirrels. Above the spring was the very large Buckshole Reservoir, known of course as the 'reservoy' and here we repaired every spring to gather frog spawn. We kept this hopefully in the back yard in jam jars and became wildly excited when the legs and tails appeared. I do not remember actually producing a fully mature frog, though there was always a reason – blame it on the cat. (Many years later when walking by myself at the side of Shornden Reservoir, a very damp shady spot also in Alexandra Park, I became aware that I had been joined by hundreds of tiny developed frogs, so thin and fragile, and all making their way uphill away from the water.

Maybe it was a group memory which told them that if they reached someone's garden and split up, their chances of survival would be increased.)

There had always been a path leading up from Buckshole into the country via the Ghyl, but no-one but the kids ever went there. (A town councillor, Mr Tingle, saw the possibilities at the time of the slump, and the unemployed were set to work on all kinds of unlikely jobs, like building paths in the glens. He also decided it would be a good thing to sort out this potentially attractive pathway, build up the side away from the steep slope, and introduce it to the public. He was hooted as a madman – no money in it – no-one would want to walk up there, and so on. He in fact won the day and an enchanting path, inevitably called Tingle's Dingle, was made along the side of Old Roar. This is now in a state of collapse, as the whole bankside consists of layers of clay and sandstone, an unsteady mixture.)

This walk to Old Roar was another of my mother's favourites (together with the path to North's Seat). Many a Sunday evening Mum, Muriel and I spent on foot, with Lionel out on his own ploys and Dad working. In those days the new path had not been made. It now runs underneath the main London road, St Helens Road, but then we had to come up for air, so to speak, and make use of the fields. Thank goodness some of the extensive woodland has been preserved by an organisation founded for that purpose. It is but a dot on the map compared with what it used to be, though still spangled with anemones, bluebells, celandines and many other flowers, and enjoyed by squirrels and birds.

## The Brassey Institute

One of the most important buildings in Hastings, at least to me, was the Brassey. Here it was free for all whenever it was open, which was every day and into the evening. Here was a place where one could come and go as one pleased as long as one's behaviour was circumspect. It had not changed at all on the exterior since it was built – it was a kind of comfortable Victorian Gothic – imposing enough to make a cultural statement, but not enough to be awe-inspiring. There were three main floors, a sufficiently impressive staircase, and a view from the top balcony along Robertson Street, past the Albert Memorial, as far as the Castle remains. This view had been pictured many times by a succession of would-be artists, for whom this was obviously set as a regular task, and very skilfully it was done. (Every now and again a sample turns up in a folio in a secondhand shop.)

This building was in Claremont, or, as we are now asked modishly to call it, the Trinity Triangle. When I was a very young child the first floor was the attraction, for this was the Municipal Museum. It was largely stocked by artifacts from all over the world, brought home in the Sunbeam, a famous yacht belonging to the Brasseys, who, having made their money from coal, preferred to spend it travelling, and made a home at Ashburnham. There were enough objects here to set the young mind racing. One of my favourites was a huge cloak made of minute feathers, worn by some chief in Australasia. There were weapons, fishing gear and clothes of every kind. Later, on the building of a new museum at the top of Cambridge Road, there was a change of stress to India and all things Indian.

Other exhibits were, inevitably, dozens of stuffed birds and small mammals, sections of sea-shore with appropriate rocks, stones, sand, seaweed, limpets and mussels. This pleased me to think I was habitually part of a museum piece. There was a picture that struck me – a lurid painting of The Scapegoat by Millais. When I had the subject explained to me, I was very, very sad. The other important and beautiful work of art was a 'Dancing Faun', just under life-size, with whom I fell hopelessly in love. (Going back at the end of the second world war to see that all was well with my childhood haunts, I found the faun was missing, and it took me a lot of questioning in many places before I learnt that a lady councillor had been so shocked – "Not even a fig leaf" – that she had had it removed and no-one knew where it was.)

The ground floor was always the Library, and this brought its own delights. I went boldly in at about eight years old and asked if I could borrow a book, please. The venerable gentleman in charge was a bit staggered and explained that I could not be a member till I was sixteen. He said, to be kind, I could come in and read when I liked, so for years I was curled up in a leather club chair, invisible to the public gaze and working my way through all of Kipling (in valuable first editions) and hundreds of other books. (The kindly Librarian was a Mr Butterfield or Butterworth, who I discovered later was somehow implicated in the Piltdown discoveries, though perhaps not an intentional participator in the original 'scam' discovered by carbon dating some years later.)

The top floor when I was very young was the School of Art, which I attended from the age of fourteen, three nights a week, till the interfering head of the grammar school I attended stopped me. She was probably right, and in any case my time would have been over-full. I was to become an art student again when my exams were over.

Many internal alterations have been made since. The Museum moved, the School of Art acquired new premises, and the whole building became a library.

# The War 1914-1918

We were not by any means untouched by the war. The day war was declared Dad came home with a full-sized tin of plain biscuits. These were for us to use when bread ran out – assuming they might see us through until the end of the war. Another time he came home from the allotment with his boots covered with mud and told us the police would be after him for stealing Lloyd George's earth. We believed him and lived in dread for several days.

Dad was de-mobbed in 1918 and, having arrived at Dover with hundreds of others, with full kit and rifle, he decided on a short cut away from all the bureaucracy. He put his rifle in the public lavatory, and hitched a lift home with the rest of his kit. I do not know what he eventually did with his uniform, but he fortunately still filled his civvy clothes. So he remained a member of the armed forces – but no one seemed interested. He always did what he wanted to do, such as going AWOL in Northern France, trekking across to Brussels, visiting the opera and returning safely through occupied Belgium.

He had a good war as a craftsman in the Royal Flying Corps and so, though just behind the firing line, he was never actually under fire. He spent his time writing signs and notices, and helping artificers in repairing crashed planes. In his plentiful spare time he made dozens of picture frames, small boxes, even buttonhooks, out of bits and pieces. I have now in front of me a painting of him in a beautifully shaped frame made from the propeller of the plane of the German Ace, Von Richtofen, which his section shot down.

Planes in those days were made of wood or lightweight metal, with very, very fine linen stretched across the frame, then treated with 'dope' to make the weave even tighter and more impermeable. Yards and yards of this stuff was always around and Dad put it to good use. He sent quite a few presents home to us, uncensored: marching chocolate, French dolls and embroidery. These things were wrapped and re-wrapped in layers of aeroplane fabric, the final layer stitched with tiny stitches and the whole thing doped. The tight fabric and small stitches meant that the censors used to pass it straight through. They were obliged to do up anything they decided to open, exactly as it was received by them, and they could not face it. I had some dresses made of aeroplane fabric, with red French knots and feather-stitching to cheer up the plain unbleached colour. We slept in sheets made from it for years, and it was not all used up until I went to college in 1927, when I had the shock of sleeping in ordinary cotton sheets, after the luxury of pure linen.

I won't enumerate all the songs we sang during this time, there were too many, Tipperary, Killarney, Roses are Blooming in Picardy, and so on, except one which we heard a lot of and sang lustily:

> "We are the men of Sussex,
> Sussex by the sea,
> We plough and sow and reap and mow
> And Sussex men are we,
> And if you go to Sussex
> Whoever you may be,
> You can tell them all that we stand or fall
> For Sussex by the sea."

The Fifth Royal Sussex Regiment became based in Hastings, and there was drilling and marching and barking of orders all over the place, particularly in our street, because of the existence of the big Drill Hall. The men drilled, ate and often slept there. They were billeted out as well on the general populace. Dad was already called up and in France, but we got three large and brawny privates to sleep and partly feed. I can't think how we slept them. It must have been two to a bed and one on the floor. Anyway they were rough but pleasant enough chaps, who were always polite and considerate. We learnt various things from them; forming fours, how to box, and how to put on puttees. This took a great deal of practice, but I got it right in the end and must have looked odd prancing about with my legs bound in khaki. We were in fact, sorry to see the soldiers go, especially as it was straight to France and then to the front line, from which so many never came back.

Life went on much as before, except that now Lionel was fourteen and tacitly treated by my mother as the man of the family, in that she pandered to his tastes in food. So dinner time might consist of anything from whelks to tinned pork and beans. These, together with plenty of plum and apple jam, and the introduction of condensed milk (which at first was sweetened), went a long way to fill our tummies. The plum and apple jam was even sung about by the troops. The only other kind was known as 'strawberry' and was made of turnips and plums and the introduction of wooden pips, to prove it was made of real strawberries.

When we had no soldiers billeted, families from London got into the habit of coming down to the town. So we made a few friends and a few nuisances. They paid for their maintenance, but slept where they could. My mother was very glad of the money, and I found myself sleeping on the floor as often as in a bed.

Opinions and arguments went on as usual in the house, and we were well trained in the hatred of the Germans. They threw babies out of upstairs windows onto bayonets held beneath. They rubbed salt into wounds as a form of torture. They boiled up the bones and bodies of dead English soldiers to extract fat and make soap. And so on.

My mother had three papier-mâché reliefs given free by Tit Bits, or John Bull, or Answers – all current journals of ordinary households – one of 'Bobby' Roberts, one of Kitchener, and one of the King of Poor Little Belgium. They were coloured to represent bronze, and remained on the kitchen wall for many years – even after the death of Kitchener. His death left everybody devastated, so that you would have thought the end of the world had come.

The much respected John Bull, to whom most readers were devoted – Horatio Bottomley – twice M.P. and newspaper proprietor and general rallyer of the people for Britain, was at last denounced as a swindler, not only of the rich, but also of the poor ordinary square-basher, and put behind bars for five years.

One bit of the war effort now surprises me, perhaps since I was so little and yet remembered it. We were told to look for St John's Wort plants, and were shown how if you held them up to the light you could see transparent blotches which were the cells which held the magic medicine. Now of course the plant has taken its place amongst all the others – garlic etc. which are guaranteed to make you live longer – at a price. As a matter of fact St John's Wort did grow in the East Hill and Ecclesbourne vicinities – but not in such vast quantities as to make much of an impression.

# Finale

The end of the first twelve years is a good time to stop. Before 1920 I was either a baby, or one of many carefree 'guttersnipes' who inhabited the central streets of the town. This expression was not as I saw myself, but as my respectable Grandma Knights, who lived in the same street, saw me. She never succeeded, the old darling, in making a lady of me, though she never gave up trying.

Looking back over this account of an enjoyable childhood, several things, which I had never before realised, stand out in my mind. First of all, what a happy and close family we were, not worried by poverty (that is something that is only understood in relation to how much the rest of your world had). The only set-backs were recurring peccadilloes of my brother Lionel, who evidently felt becoming a vicar in the Church of England later made up for his villainies as a boy. But what was a cohesive family unit had its special loyalties. Until I wrote this I didn't know how close to my father I was, and how large a figure he appears in these pages. One would have expected Lionel, the first born, especially as he was a boy, to be interested in the business, but he never seemed to be called upon to, "Take this coffin-plate home", or "Help me snap a line", or "Help me in with this glass." Of course, I not only thought it natural, but also enjoyed this arrangement.

In fact my brother was taken into the business officially at the age of twenty-odd, when he had failed to hold down various other jobs. My little

*Illustration 21 - Kit Knights aged twelve*

sister always stuck to my mother very happily. I filled my indoor time with playing cards, reading, painting, drawing, and designing alphabets. Any attempt to make a useful housewife out of me was more or less over my dead body; little Muriel was very happy fulfilling that role.

The other thing that impresses me is how a life as we lived it in the streets and at home was such a very good education. Having little money we made do in a hundred ways. Mere sticks and stones and water became our toys and we had to stretch not only our imaginations, but our organisational powers and craftsmanship.

The things we played with were never garish, perhaps dull, but at least they were natural. I include paper, of which a hundred things could be made and a hundred games invented. They varied between the very simple, like aeroplane darts, to the zoetrope which Lionel and I made at the age of 10 and 14. With the aid of a tray and some special jelly we even published a magazine, which nobody ever bought!

It was an amiable, and respectful world where, although material goods were scarce, family and community ties were paramount, and we enjoyed our freedom.

"Tomorrow to fresh woods, and pastures new"

# To My Family

Having come to the end of my childhood memories, I would like to conclude with a message to my family. I have been cheered in my maturity and old age by the continuing friendship between my sons, Andrew and Philip, and their real interest in each other's work and achievements. I would also thank my grandchildren, for whom I wrote these memoirs, for being so affectionate and caring.

I feel, as I'm in old age looking back, that the life of children has become so straightened and so restricted that, in spite of the freedom of liberal primary education and of the broadening horizons of the telly, I am sorry for many young people today, surrounded as they are by every opportunity and considerable careful indulgence; taken to school and park, brought back, unable to play out because of traffic and fear of possible molestation or attack from adults or older children, taken away on holidays, parked in play centres, they must live in an adult-hedged world with very little opportunity to build the kind of childhood which I enjoyed so much. Though of course it was not to be found everywhere, especially in that period of approaching unemployment and homelessness. Besides inventing and constructing our own world, there stretched a grey area of borrowing – cadging – scrounging – half-inching and 'finding things that had fallen off the back of a lorry', which reached its height in the first world war amongst adults as well. Nowadays there has grown a darker development, where the appropriation of property has reached right round the upper echelons of society, to become a danger to society itself.

The growth of technology has taken children far away from my primitive roots, but I doubt if it has really improved their knowledge of the world or their ability to cope with it. Nowadays, from day one, they get garishly coloured plastic objects, many of a supposed educational use, but really only for handling and looking at.

I really believe that all the space and community spirit, with which we grew up, had a lasting effect on our characters. Without putting it into words we really enjoyed the freedom. Not for nothing was the traditional Sussex hog always drawn with a caption underneath, 'Won't be druv'. Of course, the movement of populations dilutes local characteristics, but our corner of Britain has always been noted for its intransigence. This especially applies to the indigenous fishermen, who have resented and successfully resisted many of the intentions of Parliament or Council. It is also an attitude that has been shared by you, my pigheaded darlings, and perhaps by me.

By now you will have established a number of relationships outside the family, some passing and some, I expect one day, more lasting. Come what may, I do hope that you will retain your present family relationships. Go on and enjoy each other in whatever way you can.

# Addendum

Kathleen Crozier wrote the following poems and stories long before she started writing these memoirs. Rather than interrupt the flow of the story by inserting them in the main text, it was decided to include them in a separate section.

## Lament for a Space

From five o'clock on Mondays
Till dusk, or dark came down
The children of the streets around the centre of the town
Would gather in the Cricket Ground,
The lovely Central Cricket Ground,
And race and shout
And fall about
And know the cops or groundsmen could never turn them out.

From Middle Street and Station Road
And nearby Priory Street,
From Mann Street and St Andrews Square the children used to meet
To play within the Meadow,
The lovely Priory Meadow,
With ropes and balls,
With piercing calls,
And never thought they'd be turned out for flashy Shopping Malls.

## Kathleen Crozier

And now we're old or ailing,
Worn out, and full of years,
To sacrifice our memories must bring us close to tears,
To lose at last the Central Ground,
The airy Central Cricket Ground,
Instead of grass,
And room to pass,
No sound of sport – but ringing tills, and sounding brass.

*The Ground was open to the children of the surrounding streets to play in every Monday evening from 5 to 9. The writer was born in Middle Street 96 years ago, so she should know.*

It Was Like This

## Under the Pier

Under the pier it's dark and cold.
Around every red-rusted, barnacle-encrusted column
Lies a dubious pool of grey water -
How deep one cannot tell.
A cautious toe stops at the edge,
Dare not investigate the oozy depth.
It might go down and down for ever,
At least to the roots of that iron pillar
Which, struck with a stone, rings and booms
And echoes through empty naves.
In those dim depths might lurk
A sullen hermit, waving its delicate claws from within its squat,
A poison-crab with deadly syringe ready lofted,
A powerful Jack Abler, or a jelly-fish
Ready to kill at a touch.
Seaweed hangs from the crossbars above,
Dripping and dropping something foul.
Between the quiet splashings, the fall of feet
On wooden boarding overhead is faintly heard.

Big boys and brother clamber joyfully
Through disintegrating stays and stanchions,
Shouting "Follow me, I'll do yer dags."

I, myself, suddenly small and female,
Won't follow, can't follow,
But run at once from chill within the shadows
On to the warm and friendly sand
And dance in the sun alone.

Kathleen Crozier

## Down in the Govers

"Keep all together," she said as she handed out sandwiches.
"Look after Kit -
And you mustn't go down in the Govers."

Snacks snatched in transit, cresting the cliff,
Down the first glen, and up, then down to the second,
Climbing up the crumbling path again – everyday stuff,
And so we went down in the Govers.

A track through the gorse,
A drop over the side,
A climb down the rocks,
A slither, a slide,
A scrabble through thorns
Till we reached the old landslip,
A misshapen shelf torn down from the cliff.
Dwarfed blackthorn trees the height of our heads
Rooted in rocks or growing from pools of clay,
Yellow or pink or dazzling white,
Contorted and stunted by winds and sea-spray.
They tore at my hair and my ribbons, my jersey and skirt.
O.K. for the boys, tough suited, tough booted.
They stamped and they yelled, threw stones and pranced
Till I was alone.

Maybe I was scared – but high with delight as well,
For now it was all, all mine.
I stumbled about hardly able to walk,
My feet underwater, falling on boulders,
Unable to pierce the tangle of thin black twigs.
Unknown, unseen, extremely indignant birds
Clattered their wings and nattered above me.
Plantations of mare's tails like primeval forests
Broke up as I started to pick them for home,
Small creatures sped rustling through the dried grasses,

## It Was Like This

Not rabbits, not adders, they all stayed up top,
Enjoying the sandy and sun-warmed cliffs.
No – this was the wild-wood – the jungle, the waste.
This was my own.

Dirty, dishevelled and tired we came back.
"Where have you been to?" she said.
"We've been down in the Govers".
Smiling "Don't be so silly, you know NO-ONE goes down in the Govers".

That was a lifetime ago.
Those casual, comradely boys
Are wizened, or bloated, or dead like my brother.
And I'll never return to the Govers.

*Covehurst is now on the official maps. Did the cartographers thus translate our local jargon? Or did we render a civilised name in our own fashion? Which came first, the chicken or the egg?*

## A. M. Stonham

Almost the most well known character in the town from the late twenties to the early forties derived his fame by being in a tub! No, he was not a Diogenes, more like the old men of Gotham, because he too went to sea in a tub, though never more than twenty or thirty yards out.

In those pre-war days the Hastings beach in the summer was dotted all over with holiday makers, both locals and incomers, sitting on the stones enjoying the sea breezes. Moving among them, between the Old Town and the Pier would come a young fisherman rattling a wooden box and asking for pennies for the old man in the tub.

As a child, I believed Biddy Stonham to be old – to me anything above twenty was old – but looking back I see him as always the same, a biggish, strong, active man from early middle age, to old age, when I lost sight of him. He might have been a bit run to seed, but the salt of the sea and the amount of beer he consumed had him well pickled in more ways than one. His face was blunt, rubicund and sweaty, his hair cropped short and probably grizzled quite early, and I am sure his eyes were blue. He wore, in my time, an old blue sea jersey and shiny blue trousers rolled up to the knee, showing his tough sinewy legs and his prehensile toes. On his head he wore an ancient, greening top hat, slightly too big, and as he had a curious habit of making small and very rapid nodding movements it appeared to be about to fall into the sea, and sometimes did. I have a photo of him in what must have been old age, when he appears to have decorated this hat with bits and bobs of ribbons and flowers, and changed his jersey for a somewhat shapeless and flamboyant shirt. He looks at last what he really was, a clown rather than a seaman.

He started off from the harbour and propelled himself westwards with his one oar, in the manner of a coracle, amazingly swiftly. When he got to a promising beach with plenty of people – usually between the yachts and the pier – he would start his performance. He rotated his tub at enormous speed. He stood on the rim gripping with his toes and shouting in a plummy and guttural voice, "Would any young lady like to come in the tub?" He even stood on his head in it waving his feet madly in the air. Young ladies in those days were less tough and more giggly than now, but often one bold hussy would venture, often dragging her friend with her to keep up her morale. This delighted the audience and the more the flappers flapped and screeched, the more pennies clunked into the box, especially when they showed their drawers when climbing in or out. Give him his due, I never saw him tip them into the sea unless they were wearing bathing costumes. On one occasion when no more frivolous young things came forward, he took me on board, a most stolid and unmoving schoolgirl – it was a terrifying experience. When he had another body on board the tub rode very low in the water, and when he picked up two, the sea lapped over the edge and you got at least wet feet.

Biddy the tubman used to live in Union Row, one of the many groups of cottages pulled down to make room for The Bourne. I understand he never learned to read and write and it was very easy to play a trick on him. Indeed, his second wife, it is said, discovered that his boys on the beach had a habit of not handing over all the takings, so after that she organised the collections herself.

Biddy's tub and oar can still be seen in the Fishermen's Museum. There is a small café at Rock a Nore called Biddy's and there was also a suggestion that the new square in George Street should be named after him.

## The P & P Boards

Yes – you remember Station Road before the developers and the Council got at it. It was a one-sided community, facing the wall which ran along the side of the Cricket Ground, small cottages at the bottom of the road near The Clarence, and rather bigger houses at the top, near the British Legion and the Royal George. But you can't remember the P & P boards that appeared on summer Sundays at tea-time, at the end of the cottage gardens.

In those days – 1912 onwards – travel was minimal, but horse-buses and pony-traps were slowly being replaced by the combustion engine, and days out were achieved by means of a motor coach, known as a 'sharrabang'. Several of these, belonging to the pioneering Mr Timpson, lined up on the promenade to take visitors and locals to Battle Abbey, Fairlight, Wannock Tea Gardens or Bodiam Castle.

And S.E. London came in crowds to visit the sea, in fleets of charabancs which disgorged their cheerful Cockneys in various places, and picked them up again at tea-time in Station Road. The charabancs waited parked along the Cricket Ground wall, and as one loaded up and left, another took its place. On a busy sunny Sunday this going and coming went on happily, even uproariously, between about five and six-thirty.

It had become the habit of some of the merry ladies, full of stout, port and lemon, and many many cups of tea, to knock at the doors of the cottages and say, "Can I use your lavatory, please? I'll never last out till Bermondsy, or Rotherhithe or Greenwich." In those days it was not regarded as so unusual to make such a request, and it was usually answered with generosity and understanding, in the same way that a request for a drink of water at the door was always satisfied. Of course, in the town men were well catered for, there was even a smelly urinal at the bottom of the road, next to the Police Station; but for women, nothing. They were not, I suppose, acknowledged in public to have bodily functions. Often on the journey back, while the men lined up in comradely and often competitive rows at the side of the hedge, panic stricken women searched for gates and bushes behind which to manipulate their long skirts and drawers, only to return under the jeers and jolly badinage of the men with more than their spirits dampened.

Certainly after a good day at the seaside precautionary relief was necessary. But the good nature and fellow feeling of the cottagers tended to evaporate when faced with hundreds of red-faced and sometimes tipsy

Londoners milling up and down their road, searching for the right coach or the lost child. All of these were overtired, fretful, crying, clutching melting hokey-pokey, buckets of seawater containing scuttling crabs and chains of wet sea weed, and all with immortal urges.

So an ingenious cottager decided to charge a penny for the use of her convenience, always outside anyway. Others decided to take up the idea, and so the P and P board was born, and the sour little front gardens were now filled with legitimate, laughing queues.

We lived in Middle Street and tended to look down on the Station Road kids, but my Dad, a signwriter, picked up the odd shilling or two, writing tasteful wooden boards, though most notices were scrawled in pencil on disintegrating cardboard. When there was nothing more interesting to do on a summer Sunday tea-time, we went round the corner to share the excitement and the hurly-burly created by these exotic jolly Londoners, who were rich enough to pay a whole penny for a P.

# In the Hop Gardens

One day recently the face of Aunt Louie – Louie Kemp – appeared in my mind's eye for no reason that I could think of – as large as life, and twice as natural. Yet I had neither seen her, nor even thought about her since I was a child. She must have been dead for at least fifty years by now. It was a strong face, almost masculine, made of soft brown leather, much wrinkled and folded, and always smiling, showing strong white teeth, below eyes like ripe blackberries. Her clothes were dark and nondescript, and she always wore a shapeless black felt hat.

She seems to have been a long standing friend of my Grandmother Knights. We never knew how this sturdy countrywoman came to know my neat and ladylike little grandma, with her tidy lavender blouses and lace collars and her widow's bonnet decorated with jet bugles. Louie came into town by train once a week to shop. She took tea with Grandma, admired her aspidistra and counted its leaves again. Thirty nine was its highest score, and it was always stood out on the pavement when it drizzled, so that passers by could admire. She would then cross the street to our house to say "Hallo". We, the children, liked her very much, though she never brought any sweets, nor attempted to ingratiate herself with attentions. I suppose we appreciated her dignity and cheerfulness, and the very smell of the country that she brought with her.

She lived at Brede, a pretty village six or seven miles out of town. Very occasionally in the summer we went to visit her, taking a tram to the back of the town and walking the rest of the way. Her cottage was nearly opposite the church and would now be considered worthy of a picture postcard. Once when we arrived she was standing by her gate in a cotton pinafore, wearing a real old-fashioned sun-bonnet, sprigged with flowers, corded and ruched, and with long strings. I was so obviously charmed that she promised, if only she could get hold of a bit of stuff, she would make me one. It never came my way, and I was rather relieved that I was not to have the choice of not wearing it and offending her, or wearing it and feeling embarrassed.

Once I was left to stay the night. There were spiders in the corner of the bedroom, which let themselves down on long threads from the thatch above my head. The bees cruised alarmingly among the honeysuckle which almost engulfed the doors and windows, but I did not like to show my fear. I did not care for the lavatory much, either. It was a donikin at the bottom of the garden, furnished with a bucket of earth, and a small shovel and old copies of the Argus, sliced small and strung on a string. The hole was much too big for my small bottom, so that I had to hang on tight lest I should descend into the pit, which, as far as I knew, could be bottomless. Besides, what might live down there?

The next day Aunt Louie took me across to the church to do the flowers, taken from her garden. Then she showed me Dean Swift's cradle. Though already a great reader, I did not know who Dean Swift was, but thought the wooden trough looked cold and uncomfortable. I hoped the poor little baby would soon grow too big for it, and be taken into its parents' bed – in my experience the normal place for a baby. She showed me, too, the Effigy of the Giant of Brede Place, who roamed the fields and used to eat little children. I hoped he had not eaten little Dean Swift and was relieved to see that he was now immovable and made of stone. Sir Giles Oxenburgh looked uncomfortable but imposing in his armour, though not nearly as big as other giants I had seen in pantomimes, whose Fee Fi Fo Fums came rumbling out from the region of their stomachs.

Our friendship with Louie Kemp came to a head every September. She earned some extra money then by having a bin in the hop-gardens, which paid better than her other odd jobs. It was very hard work, though enjoyable. The hop gardens round us in those days were very small affairs. They belonged to individual farmers, who planted the hops, tended them, packed them, and sold the full pokes to the brewers. Nowadays the brewers own everything. Then they stuck to their brewing and bought their hops from the accredited markets at Maidstone or Canterbury, or even from the main Hop Exchange in Southwark. All the picking around Brede was done by the locals, or by incomers and friends from Hastings. There was no descent of the South East Londoners, no hopping camps, no knees-ups at the pubs on a Saturday night. That was for Kent, and would have horrified seemly Sussex, bringing with it all those lousy, noisy, scrumping kids.

The ground was cultivated by hand or by horse nidget (I never knew what this was), and well mulched. The fields from Brede to the coast had once been underwater from the sea and the rivers Brede and Tillingham. All those little villages whose names end in 'ey' were once islands. The land near the sea remained interlaced with dykes, fit only for the famous Romney Marsh sheep. Further inland is the low moist soil in which the hops delighted.

In winter, before the new growth took place, we loved to see the men stringing the poles, each stuck in a small mound. Sometimes permanent wires steadied the tops, and then coarse coconut string stretched from ground to top, fanning out like an inverted steeple, so that as the bines grew they could get plenty of sun and air and the fruit could form.

Above the windward hedge was mounted a coarse canvas windbreak, seven or eight feet high. In April the young bines would start to shoot – the men would scrape away some of the soil to expose the crowns. The old bines would be trimmed to within an inch or two, or destroyed. Promising buds would be cut out and re-planted to make new sets. As the shoots curled up towards the light the village women came to do the first tying in, often with dried rushes from the Tillingham. This was repeated several times during the period of growth.

Then we could smell the fish manure, replacing the old warm smell of the turned earth, and later still the smell of the tobacco spray to kill the aphids; and we could see the sulphur dust puffing between the plants. We still had to wait months for the true smell of the hop gardens. The time we liked best was when, at the last tying in, the men came into their own again and walked about the gardens on stilts, repairing wind damage, and sorting out and gathering in the waving tops of the bines. By now these were overgrowing the poles, searching for support, joining up with the next door plants or even growing back down on their own strings. All this would make harvesting very difficult, and put the bin men in a nasty temper as they tried to separate the plants and bring them down to the bins without losing too much fruit.

By midsummer the green hops were beginning to form and their smell was everywhere, bitter and delicious. As they ripened, passers-by pulled a handful when no one was about, to stuff pillows to make them sleep, or to brew soporific infusions. It was said that some had earlier stolen young shoots to boil, like spinach or nettles. Soon there was hardly a house in the village or town which had not a swathe of hops draped somewhere in the kitchen. Children nibbled them, wrinkled their noses and spat them out, wondering why their parents set so much store by the bitter stuff, or by beer either.

Ah! but September was the month! The green of the gardens was punctuated with colour, the quiet enlivened by activity and buzzing with gossip. Families or groups of friends were allotted bins, two adults and two or three children. These last helped intermittently and often disappeared into the surrounding fields and woods. Only if their mother was poor enough or forceful enough did they work consistently. The women wore sackcloth aprons and bright cotton overalls which soon became black. Their heads were shielded by old straw hats and sunbonnets. They started in the morning mists with old jerseys, or even sacks around their shoulders and gradually shed layers as the sun rose higher and the grey air turned to gold. The children picked, or visited other families, or disappeared till lunch time. They were seldom uproarious and never ran. A certain decorum was demanded, with poles and bins and sacks all over the ground, and trolleys and bin men and tallymen all on the move. The women's hands were black in no time, and often cracked by the end of the day.

So once a year we would spend what was always for me one of my happiest times – a whole day in the hop garden. I cannot remember it ever raining – perhaps we only set out when the weather was fine. It seems now that it always was in those days. We all got up early. My mother cut a huge pile of sandwiches. We walked up to the station and took a little local train to Doleham Halt, or Three Oaks or Guestling, which ever was the nearest to the farm where Aunt Louie was picking. The train would stop for us when we asked the driver and we got down on what was not more than a short path with a wooden bench. We went out through the swing gate and through the water meadows for a mile or two, picking blackberries and rather unripe crack nuts, or the somewhat fading meadowsweet.

When we had located Louie's bin and been greeted with a huge sparkling grin, Mum put on her apron and picked faithfully all day except at sandwich time. We all started with enthusiasm, but were so often reprimanded for picking by handfuls and so dropping leaves into the bin – a cardinal sin – that my brother and I soon wandered off. We left my sleepy baby sister tied to a hop pole by a scarf, so that when she woke up she could not toddle away and get trodden on. My father lasted scarcely longer, but sauntered up the hill towards the village, leaning on every other gate to enjoy his pipe, and only stopping when he reached the local pub.

The men cut down the bines and brought them to the bins. They carried away the stripped ones and dumped them temporarily at the edge of the field. When dry they might be used for silage or animal litter, or even to make a base for straw or corn stacks. The bins were simply lengths of hessian with poles slotted into the long sides and fitted on to a tripod of poles at each end. When you thought your bin was full the overman came and thumped his two fists into it – pressing hard to prove it was really scarcely more than half full – and that, anyway, there were so many leaves and stalks in it he might not feel like passing it. The men bullied the women mildly and the women bullied the children and older helpers somewhat more fiercely. When the bin was really full it was unhooked and carted away to be weighed and entered in your tally. All our pickings, of course, went into Louie Kemp's account.

Lionel and I wandered off through the nearby fields, stuffed ourselves with blackberries and the small, rather green, cracknuts, climbed a few trees, shouted joyfully when we found mushrooms for our parents, and lay in the sun. I shall never forget once opening my eyes to see, crossing the bottom of the field, slowly and elegantly, a white sail. This must surely be magic, a fairy boat which travelled through grass. It was not till many weeks afterwards that my scornful brother pointed out that the River Brede ran across the bottom of the field, with a high bank which completely hid the boat. For me, always, remained the vision of the fairy sail, like a white butterfly, skimming above a Sussex meadow.

With Dad back from the pub, we two back from the fields, the baby awake and the sandwiches unwrapped, even the lunch was unforgettable. Our hands were so impregnated with the bitter oil that the food was flavoured too, and not knowing whether we liked the bitterness or not, we ploughed into those sandwiches – our ravenous consumption approved by our mum – after all, the hops were very medicinal.

After lolling in the sun and wandering the hedges Lionel and I would try to get into the oast house. Some years we did, some years we were unlucky. It all depended on the good nature of the drier and packer. We would climb tentatively up the open rough wooden steps on the outside, to the drying floor. Inside, the whole air was swimming with golden motes of hop-dust – sometimes so thick we would make masks with our handkerchieves, though I never saw the men wear such a thing. One end of the first floor of the oast was slatted with lathes about a quarter of an inch apart, and covered with a rough horse hair or hop sacking. Here the hops were piled up and underneath was the furnace, sometimes of cast iron, sometimes of brick, and a low heat was constantly kept up twenty hours a day – depending on the size of the harvest. Wood, turf or charcoal was burned, as coal smoke would taint the hops. We were threatened that if we set a toe off the solid floor and on to the hopsacking we would fall through, get roasted and packed in a hop-poke. The hops were shovelled green from floor to hopsack and spread some six inches deep. They were kept moving by wide wooden shovels, or sometimes by a hopsack fixed to a wooden frame rather like a shrimping net. Great care was taken not to overheat or cook the hops, and they must still be greenish when finished. A practised eye knew when to shove them away up the other end to cool off and make way for the next batch.

We used fairly soon to tire of the heat and the dust-laden, almost choking, atmosphere and go back down the steps to the open ground floor. This part of the process I liked to watch best. At the cool end of the oast, if we looked up, we could see large round holes, some empty and showing a slightly larger ring of iron just above them, to which pockets would be temporarily sewn with coarse twine, or fixed with tenterhooks. Other holes might have the long poke hanging loosely and waiting to be filled, some might be half-filled like deflated sausages, and we could watch them slowly swelling out from the bottom up and becoming giant taut cylinders as the cured hops were swept into them. These monsters, six foot tall, held 10 bushels and weighed about 1½ cwt. In the old days, said the dryer, little boys were employed to stand inside and stamp down the hops, but my brother never accepted the offer of a job, especially when one packer friend hinted that sometimes the boys were overcome by the dust and never re-appeared. After all, dead rats are said to be used to improve the quality of cider, so why not have dead boys in beer? "And what a lovely death," said our informer, as he used a wooden lever to tamp the poke solid. When ready the poke was detached from its ring, sewn tight at the top, marked with its weight, its grower's name, parish and county badge which bore a crowned shield with the six martlets. These were birds with no feet, which worried us a lot. We were told that the next county was marked with the Kentish horse. Then up went the pockets. At the end of the season they used up some rather battered ones, as they said, "Good canvas for good hops, rough hemp for late, discoloured hops."

These men were not driven to furious activity as many of the bin men and tellers were, and had time to gossip and tell us about the old times – when they could tell the different strains of hops, with names like Tolhurst from Horsmonden; Bramlings and Fuggles from the stiff land behind; along with Goldings and Canterbury Jacks, Golden Tips and Pretty Willis, Rufflers, Apple Puddings and Warings Imperial. Now they all seemed the same. They talked about how, when the war was over, the law said 50% of the hops were to be grubbed up. Already, before 1914, foreign hops had been coming in – poor stuff full of leaves and stalks, sand, straw and loggets of wood. Some men had even been asked to tip them out of their pokes and re-bag them in British sacks. "There's good hops, wild hops and unkindly hops, but these foreigners were dross of other sorts," said our informant.

Time passed quickly around the oast houses, but we were eventually chased back to the hop garden itself. We heard the whistle blown to say "Pull no more bines." The bin men chivvied the pickers to hurry and finish the poles they already had. The measurers were no longer so careful to bash down the bin full. The tally man put the last file marks across the 16 inch tally sticks which were divided into two halves, one for the picker and one for himself, or he would write the tally in his book. Books were gradually ousting the sticks as the education in the little country schools became less interrupted or shortened by farm-work, and reading and writing became less bothersome.

Everybody now would be packing up. The women took off their pinafores, now stained and stiffened, took up their baskets and the hands of their sun-baked and weary children and trailed up the hill to the village. There they would start work all over again to prepare a meal for the men when they arrived. Nobody would need sleeping pills. By the time supper was done they were drugged by the sun and fresh air; by the hop dust and the odd glass of beer.

The Knights family packed its bits and pieces, said goodbye and thanks to Aunt Louie and made slowly for the Halt. One occasion I shall not forget is when my little sister, who was about two, ate a large ripe pear as the clearing-up started. Unfortunately a wasp decided to share it and Muriel Stella was stung on the tongue, which swelled alarmingly. My mum panicked and was sure the child would choke to death – I was silently terrified. Aunt Louie, calm as ever, produced a Reckift's blue bag from her basket to rub the sting. So we went in the train with a blue faced baby, who seemed more comfortable now. All the way home the train said, "Don't let the baby die, don't let the baby die, don't let the baby die."

And she didn't.

Printed in the United Kingdom
by Lightning Source UK Ltd.
101636UKS00002B/265-297